*With heart, honesty ...
offering of a peek in...
of the craziness of ...
along your own path ... ...*
and truth, this is a boo... ... ...*Catholic who ever
lived in a family will appreciate.*

Lisa M. Hendey, Founder of CatholicMom.com
and author of *The Grace of Yes*

Everyday Sacrament *is a gift to every parent
everywhere. Whether she's writing about giving
a newborn a bath or flying with a cranky toddler,
Fanucci reveals the holiness that lives right in the
mess of parenting. Her writing is graceful, sensitive,
and honest in its portrayal of the highs and lows of
motherhood. This beautiful book is a feast for the
mind, the heart, and the soul.*

Ginny Kubitz Moyer, author of *Random
MOMents of Grace: Experiencing God in the
Adventures of Motherhood*

Everyday Sacrament *is a gift to any of us seeking God in
the messiness of life and raising kids. With refreshing
honesty, Laura Kelly Fanucci shares her home and
heart to reveal the sacred in everything from changing
diapers to rocking a child to sleep. Along the way,
she develops a real-world theology that brings the
sacraments to life and honours parenting for the holy
vocation that it is. As with any encounter of grace,
gratitude is in order for this powerful testimony to
the messy grace of parenting.*

Jeremy Langford, author of *Seeds of Faith: Practices
to Grow a Healthy Spiritual Life* and father of three

Laura Kelly Fanucci works part-time in theological research for the Collegeville Institute at Saint John's University in Minnesota where she earned a Master of Divinity degree. Her books include *Mercy: God's Nature, Our Challenge* and *Living Your Discipleship: Seven Ways to Express Your Deepest Calling*, which she co-authored with Kathleen Cahalan. She blogs about faith and family life at Mothering Spirit: motheringspirit.com.

✮ Laura Kelly Fanucci ✮

EVERYDAY SACRAMENT

The Messy Grace of Parenting

VERITAS

Published 2018 by
Veritas Publications
7–8 Lower Abbey Street
Dublin 1, Ireland
publications@veritas.ie
www.veritas.ie

ISBN 978 1 84730 840 5

10 9 8 7 6 5 4 3 2 1

This book was originally published in English by Liturgical Press, Saint John's Abbey, Collegeville, Minnesota 56321, USA, and is published in this edition by licence of Liturgical Press. All rights reserved.

Scripture texts in this work are taken from the New Revised Standard Version Bible © 1989, Division of Christian Education of the National Council of the Churches of Christ in the United States of America. Used by permission. All rights reserved.

Excerpts from the English translation of Rite of Baptism for Children © 1969, International Commission on English in the Liturgy Corporation (ICEL); excerpt from the English translation of Rite of Confirmation © 1975, ICEL; excerpt from the English translation of Rite of Penance © 1974, ICEL; excerpt from the English translation of Pastoral Care of the Sick: Rites of Anointing and Viaticum © 1982, ICEL; excerpt from the English translation of Rite of Marriage © 1969, ICEL; excerpt from the English translation of Rites of Ordination of a Bishop, of Priests, and of Deacons © 2000, 2003, ICEL. All rights reserved.

Excerpts from the English translation of the Catechism of the Catholic Church for use in the United States of America copyright © 1994, United States Catholic Conference, Inc. Libreria Editrice Vaticana. English translation of the Catechism of the Catholic Church: Modifications from the Editio Typica copyright © 1997, United States Catholic Conference, Inc. Libreria Editrice Vaticana. Used with permission.

Translation of 'In All Things' by St Francis of Assisi from the Penguin publication *Love Poems from God: Twelve Sacred Voices from the East and West* by Daniel Ladinsky. Copyright © 2002 Daniel Ladinsky and used with his permission.

A catalogue record for this book is available from the British Library.

Designed by Padraig McCormack, Veritas Publications
Printed in Ireland by Walsh Colour Print, Kerry

For our children

It was easy to love God in all that was beautiful.
The lessons of deeper knowledge, though,
instructed me to embrace God in all things.

St Francis of Assisi, translated by Daniel Ladinsky,
Love Poems from God: Twelve Sacred
Voices from the East and West

CONTENTS

Introduction
BEFORE BEGINNING: AN UNEXPECTED STORY

The seven sacraments touch all the stages and all the
  important moments of Christian life:
they give birth and increase, healing and mission to the
  Christian's life of faith.

  Catechism of the Catholic Church, 1210

I never expected to be here.

I never expected to have children at all during our years of infertility, as I plunked box after box of pregnancy tests into my shopping cart, only to have them turn up negative again and again, month after month.

And even when a baby miraculously arrived and it seemed our prayers had been answered, I still never expected that parenting could change everything I knew about seeking God. Especially when I was so overwhelmed by new motherhood's demands that I could barely string two coherent thoughts together.

When my first son was three months old, I read a magazine article by a mother who sang praises of the beauty of babyhood and practically squealed about how close to God she felt when she gazed into her newborn's eyes. I glanced up from the magazine's glossy pages to the foggy mirror of the bathroom where I had locked myself to treat my raw, bleeding breasts with the slather of ointments my doctor promised would clear up the latest round of an agonising thrush infection passed to me by my nursing babe. I hadn't slept more than two hours in a row for twelve weeks, a stupefying stretch of sleep deprivation that threatened to violate the Geneva Convention. And the shrieking screams from the next room reminded me that it was time once again to grit my teeth and curl my toes as I tried to nurse the hungry baby through shooting pain.

I tossed the magazine in the wastebasket as I left the bathroom. I had zero interest in finding transcendence through motherhood.

But months slipped by, as months do even in that early stretch of dragging days. Gradually I started to sleep a little more. The evil thrush finally healed. The world shifted back into focus like the slow turn of a telescope. Parenthood wasn't pretty pastels and it wasn't an easy elegy, but eventually I found myself settling into mothering.

Then I began to wonder where God might be.

For a lifelong Catholic with a freshly minted degree in theology, trying to find God in the midst of my new life as a parent should have been easy. It was decidedly not.

Although I had spent three years in graduate school studying how to understand God, I suddenly felt clueless about how to seek the presence of God that I needed to survive this overwhelming transition to parenthood. I knew plenty of ways to define God intellectually, but I was scrambling to feel God's strength surrounding me when I craved it most. I had thought motherhood was my calling – a way God was inviting me to give my life in service out of love – but now it seemed the rocky path I'd chosen was far from a smooth road to spiritual enlightenment.

For starters, motherhood magnified my flaws to the nth degree: impatience, irritability, a temper that stomped its feet whenever I didn't get my way. Furthermore, every spiritual practice I'd been taught required peace, quiet, and time apart from the rush of daily life. Finding even one of these conditions – let alone all three at once – seemed impossible with a new baby at the centre of my life. Most days I barely muddled through, but whenever I found a rare moment to reflect on how unbalanced my life had become, I knew I had to find another way.

So I began to ask what it might mean to approach parenting itself as a spiritual practice. Could these long hours heaped with burp cloths reveal some spark of God's presence? Could all those dirty diaper changes hold an encounter with the divine?

One afternoon, as I rocked and rocked my wide-eyed baby in a futile search for his nap, I started thinking about sacraments. Maybe we had just come home from Mass that morning, or maybe the mail had brought yet another wedding invitation from a college friend. Whatever the reason, the idea of sacrament stuck itself in my head and wouldn't let go.

In the Catholic Church there are seven sacraments: baptism, confirmation, Eucharist, reconciliation, anointing of the sick, marriage, and holy orders. In each sacrament, we receive a visible sign of God's love for us. We are invited to enter more deeply into our relationship with God. And we are welcomed and embraced by the Church, a community that shares our celebration. Sacraments are moments of encounter when God touches, strengthens and heals us. Through the tangible things of this earth – water, oil, bread, and wine – God comes to us, giving us what we need when we open our hearts to receive.

I started to wonder if sacraments might hold the key to my mothering muddles.

As a Catholic schoolgirl I used to tick off the seven sacraments on my fingers to memorise them for religion class. I mentally checked the ones I'd received – baptism, Eucharist, reconciliation and confirmation. I calculated that I'd add marriage one day, maybe anointing of the sick when I got old, never holy orders since I wouldn't be a priest. Then my own list would be complete. Sacraments would always be the standard stuff of church, but nothing earth-shattering. Nothing to rock my world.

Until, as that bleary-eyed new mom rocking the baby over and over, I started to notice how the ordinary could be holy. And as I began to see the sacred in the everyday, I stumbled into the surprising truth of what the sacraments really meant: *that God was present always, even in the mess of new motherhood.*

When I first became a parent, I never expected that I would learn more about baptism from a baby's bath time – or about Communion from the chaos of family dinner, or about ordination from overwhelming loads of laundry – than I had from years of study that schooled me in theology or all those Sundays spent sitting in the church pews. But parenting proved to be an on-the-ground education in how sacraments spring from everyday life. Sacred encounters with God weren't limited to celebrations in church or a one-time date on the calendar. Baptism, confirmation, Eucharist, reconciliation, anointing of the sick, marriage, and holy orders – these seven experiences were lived out each day that I washed and fed and cared for my family. Through the busy, blurry years of raising young children, I was learning over and over again how sacraments received in church were deepened and strengthened through ordinary life at home. God surprised me during the endless tasks of parenting with moments of undeserved love and deep joy, with the peace to forgive and the gift of being forgiven, with a profound sense of meaning and purpose.

Theologians call this truth the 'domestic church': that we first learn about God within our experience of family life. Catholics call this perspective a 'sacramental imagination': that God is present throughout creation, all around us. I simply call it the story of how I met God as a mother: day-by-day, by surprise, and full of grace.

—⁓—

This book looks at each of the seven Catholic sacraments as a lens through which ordinary moments of raising children reflect a whole new – even holy – meaning. It is not the typical Sunday school catechesis, since it starts from the mess of lived experience rather than the beauty of Church doctrine. But everyday chaos with little ones offers its own rich theology: a thousand chances to ask *who is God?* and *who are we?* as we stumble through learning to love each other at home. Even in ordinary moments, family life can embody Pope Francis' prayer: 'I thank God that many families, which are far from considering themselves perfect, live in love, fulfilling their calling and keep moving forward, even if they fall many times along the way' (*Amoris Laetitia*, 57).

Whether you are Catholic or not, whether you are struggling with the faith in which you were raised or searching for a new way to think about God, the sacraments invite all of us to open our eyes to a wider view in which every moment offers opportunities to encounter God's grace. Since the seven sacraments celebrate what generations of Christians have learned of God's love through their daily experiences, my hope is to help turn the spotlight from concentrated moments at church to a broader view of everyday life as sacramental.

Henri Nouwen wrote in *Beyond the Mirror* that his 'deepest vocation is to be a witness to the glimpses of God I have been allowed to catch'. As a writer and a mother, this is what I try to do: to notice God at work around me and to nudge others to ask, *Do you see this, too?* Christianity has always been a faith of sharing stories, back to Jesus spinning parables about baking bread and sweeping floors and forgiving children. Through the stories gathered here, I hope that you, the reader, will find echoes of your own life, whatever your family's background, situation or experience may be. Because sacraments do not exist apart from the complexity and diversity of our daily life: they are a part of it.

These stories of sacrament are tales from the beginning of one family's life together. The wise assure me that parenting's questions and challenges will only continue to change and become more complicated as my children grow. But this book honours the truths gathered along the way, between the new parents' pride in discovering how their three-day-old likes to be held and the third-time-around veterans' shrug that every child is different. While the stories I share are limited to my own experience of becoming a mother, I believe in the importance of telling truth about our individual lives. So this book offers what I have learned along my journey and invites you to explore how you have glimpsed God in your own life. As Pope Francis writes, 'The Lord's presence dwells in real and concrete families, with all their daily troubles and struggles, joys and hopes' (*Amoris Laetitia*, 315).

Before I had kids, I never expected any of this – how God could be found so powerfully in the exasperating everyday, how home could feel as holy as church, how seven sacraments could strengthen and transform parenting. But that's how grace gets spilled: right before our eyes.

If we only stop to see it.

Part 1
BEGINNINGS: BAPTISM AND CONFIRMATION

Beginnings shape us. Each family's story opens with a first chapter: how the parents met and fell in love. Every baby has a birth story: how the labour began and when the moment of delivery arrived. A child's story of Christian faith starts with a choice made by parents and an action of the Church: the cleansing ritual of baptism, whether by sprinkling with holy water or full immersion into the baptismal font, and a warm welcome into the community of believers.

Beginnings take time. Catholics celebrate three sacraments of initiation – baptism, Eucharist, and confirmation. Each is a step in the process of becoming part of the Body of Christ that is the Church, with Christ as its head.

Typically the preparation and celebration of these three sacraments of initiation take place over the span of many years through childhood and youth. Becoming a Catholic Christian is no quick splash of water, but a process that unfolds slowly into a lifelong journey.

Beginnings are complex. Baptism is not a superstition that will magically save the child or an excuse to celebrate a new baby with another party. Confirmation is not a teenager's graduation from faith formation. Instead these sacraments are ancient rites of initiation that deepen one's relationship with God and with the Church.

Beginnings are unique. Baptism and confirmation are unrepeatable, like witnessing the birth of a child or becoming a parent for the first time. But if beginnings are left in the memory of dusty photo albums, they fade to mere moments, confined to church or childhood. Only when we return to our beginnings, explore their importance, plunge into their depths, and watch their impact rippling out in widening circles, do we start to live out what they mean.

Beginnings matter. For the life of a family and the life of faith, the rest of the story cannot unfold without them. So we tell these tales over and over again, to remember how it all got started.

CHAPTER ONE

Bathed in New Life – Baptism

SOFTENED WITH SHOWERS

You visit the earth and water it, you greatly enrich it ...
You water its furrows abundantly, settling its ridges,
softening it with showers, and blessing its growth.

Psalm 65:9, 10

Exhausted, I step into the shower, yanking the curtain behind me. The baby is sleeping at last. Silence on the monitor. I crank the silver handle to hot and slip back under the water's flow. I sigh. Alone at last.

As I suds shampoo through my greasy hair, long strands slide through my fingers and slip down the drain. Yet another postpartum perk to add to my sagging stomach and tender scars. No one told me the exhaustion of new motherhood would make me feel like a stranger in my own skin. Or that a daily shower would become a dream of the past. Or that hours to myself would be reduced to minutes.

Under the spray of the showerhead I start to wallow in self-pity. I'm tired and aching and overwhelmed by all that my newborn demands of me. I know it's the oldest story in the book, but it's the first time it's been my story. And it's hard.

Until, soft and steady as the warm water rolling down my tired shoulders, another presence whispers. Something reminds me I am not alone.

———

Only a few weeks into a calling that will last the rest of my life, I am still clueless in many ways about the challenges that motherhood will bring. While I'm already learning that parenting is not about self-fulfilment – that babies aren't all bliss, that our culture's pursuit of happiness does not equate with the deeper joys of raising children – there is still much I do not know. I don't know about the depression that lies ahead, or the unexpected loss of an unborn child, or the day-to-day drain of caring for multiple children around the clock.

But I do know the heartache of wanting a baby. I know the struggle of carrying a pregnancy. I know the pain of labour and delivery. I have learned what it means, in the words of a Caribbean saying that a friend told me, that in bearing and birthing a child, you go down to hell and wrestle with death and come out with new life.

So even now, amateur and overwhelmed, I understand a sliver of what this new life and love will demand. Over and over I will have to face my deepest fears, I will take a deep breath, and I will push through again.

Maybe we are always remembering ourselves back into this same truth that Christ taught: dying to self, rising to new life. Maybe this is what makes transformation sacred.

Maybe this is the strength of a sacrament.

I have no memory of my own baptism, more than thirty years ago.

Faded photographs show a wide-eyed baby bundled in a long white gown, my grinning siblings-turned-godparents standing next to my parents near the baptismal font. As a teenager I discovered my yellowed candle tucked in the back of a kitchen drawer. Baptism was never something special that we commemorated growing up. You were simply baptised, and that was that.

But when it came time to have my first baby baptised, everything changed.

Suddenly the sacrament loomed as a daunting prospect: a living, breathing, lifelong commitment I would be professing on behalf of a squawking six-week-old. What would initiation into the Church mean for my little son? Was I ready for this? Was he? Could any of us embrace what it really means to follow Christ?

Hosting fifty friends and relatives for the brunch after Mass quickly seemed like cake by comparison.

When I think of baptism in centuries past, I picture cavernous pools in cold stone churches. Catechumens stepping down into the cool water of the font, climbing up drenched and dripping, and then clothed in clean white garments like a newborn wrapped in blankets after birth.

Over the years I will watch as each of my babies gets plunged into those same waters, wailing from surprise at the shock of cold on their naked skin. In our parish's tradition of baptising babies by full immersion, strong hands will lift them from my arms, dip their wriggling bodies into the font, wrap them in soft white towels, and smear their smooth foreheads with sweet-smelling chrism – a mixture of oil and balsam blessed for use in sacred rites.

An ancient tradition that makes them new Christians.

Perhaps it is echoes of these memories – baptisms of earlier believers, the baptisms of my own children – that will continue to draw me back to the water, reminding me of my first and deepest identity.

———— ∿ ————

As months pass and motherhood starts to feel less foreign, I stick to my practice of starting the day – OK, every other day, if I'm lucky – with a hot shower.

Sometimes I bumble through the routine of washing my hair, still bleary-eyed from lack of sleep. Sometimes I take an extra five minutes to shave my legs, trying to ignore the baby who starts to fuss in the next room. Once in a while I cry quietly when the exhaustion is too much and I'm overwhelmed by the demands of another long day dawning.

But no matter the mood, I steal time for this ritual because – strange as it sounds – the shower bubbles up memories of baptism. These few moments to myself, wrapped in water and warmth, remind me I am a child of God before I am a mother of anyone else. Something deep in the memory of my bones craves this comfort in the simple wash of water on skin.

It might sound silly – a shower as spiritual exercise? – but whenever I close my eyes and dip my head back to meet the water, I hear echoes of belovedness, of acceptance, of forgiveness. I let yesterday's failures slip down the drain. And if I'm lucky, when I crank the handle to stop the water's flow, even the baby's whines on the monitor will not grate on my nerves as before.

I step out renewed.

PRELUDE TO BAPTISM

Through the Holy Spirit, Baptism is a bath that purifies,
justifies, and sanctifies.

Catechism of the Catholic Church, 1227

Terry washcloth. Hooded towel. Plastic bathtub. Baby shampoo. Water warmed to a perfect ninety-eight degrees. Even a camera to capture the quintessential moment. We have everything we need for our baby's first bath.

I am completely terrified.

Bathing kids was always the babysitting chore I skipped if the parents didn't care. I feared I'd break them, let them fall, or slip shampoo into their eyes, and they would dissolve into tears or tantrums or worse.

When we registered as expectant parents for the requisite tiny washcloths and ducky towels, it never registered with pregnant me that I might one day be responsible for bathing the recipient of such adorable bath-time gear. Not until the stern head nurse in the level two nursery led me over to the giant baby warmer – where our tiny son lay, with the pneumothorax trap of air caught in his lungs, with every scrawny limb taped to twisted lines leading to an army of looming monitors – and announced to me brusquely, 'He needs a bath. Are you ready?'

Oh no, I thought. This baby is three weeks early. He's not even supposed to be here yet, let alone hooked up to all these giant beeping machines while I'm stuck in an empty recovery room at the quiet end of the maternity ward.

No, I am not ready.

But I gulped down the lump of fear rising in my throat, forced a meagre smile, and started helping the nurse unwind Sam's skinny arms and legs from his tangled web of IVs. I was convinced one wrong move would jeopardise his life. But the nurse seemed exasperated enough with my cautious clumsiness that I tried to trust this bathing business would be safe.

She handed me a small square of gauze and a basin of warm, soapy water. 'Just a sponge bath for now,' she directed. 'Start with the head and move down. Don't take too long or he'll get cold.'

Then, catching the terror in my eyes, she added, 'You'll be fine.'

I nodded. And as I wet the cloth and began to dab gingerly at Sam's soft blonde hair, his tiny swirls of ears, his miniature nose, I marvelled at how he accepted my offering. Sure, he squirmed, even though he lay under the red glow of heat lamps hovering above the bassinet to regulate his temperature. But with each dip of the cloth back in the bubbly basin, his limbs relaxed with the touch of warm and wet.

Of course, I realised – one of those new-parent moments of obvious insight. The bath reminds him of where he's been for nine months: warm, wet and safe.

Much to my shock, the hospital staff eventually let us take our baby home. It seemed a wildly reckless move as we slowly inched the car out of the hospital car park without a single professional in tow. I panicked that his heart rate would suddenly plummet without the warning chorus of monitors around him, that he would starve without the nurses making regular rounds to check his cries, that he would stop breathing without the whole staff of specialists waiting to leap into action. Thank God, my husband Franco was blessed with a calm, collected presence and he settled us comfortably into our home, tenderly unwrapping the baby from his car seat, setting up the bassinet and baby monitor still stashed in their boxes, bringing me glasses of ice water as I tried to figure out how to nurse the hollering newborn. When the sun peeked over the horizon, I was stunned to find that we had all survived the first night by ourselves. I started to ease into the idea that Franco and I might actually be able to do this parenting thing on our own.

Until it came time for baby's first real bath.

I dragged my feet, putting it off for well over two weeks after we brought Sam home. Sponge baths were fine, his paediatrician had assured us. But once his umbilical cord fell off, she gently suggested that a real bath might be in order.

So we gathered the necessary provisions. I mustered all the courage I could summon. I even faked a smile for my mother, who was present to photograph the moment for his baby book.

And then I quickly handed the baby off to his father. Without a single worry Franco slid Sam's small body into the splash of the bathwater. I marvelled at how their eyes met in quiet consent. They were both at ease, undisturbed by my nervous hovering above them. I stepped back to let them be, to let them relax together in the comfort of the warmth where their hands met.

From that day forward, bath time became Franco's domain. He never worried that the water was too cold or the baby too cranky. With a calm confidence, he would rest the wriggling, slippery newborn in the crook of his strong arm, gently swabbing him with a soapy washcloth. He held Sam with the same certainty on the day he was baptised, grinning down at the baby in his arms while the priest prayed a blessing over the father of this child. Such simple, sure support.

EVERYDAY SACRAMENT

As time went on, I learned to share the bathing responsibilities, supporting Sam's wobbly neck, tending to his delicate skin, keeping shampoo suds from streaming into his eyes. And Sam learned to relax into my arms, too. Floating peacefully in the warm water that felt like home.

Years after those first baths I watch Sam, now towering as a towhead over his brown-haired younger brother Thomas. It is the Sunday after Easter, and both boys peer over the pew as our pastor rolls up his long sleeves to dip a pine branch in a bowl of water and fling its drenching spray across the congregation. Sam and Thomas shake in shock when the water splashes their faces. I laugh to myself – not just at their blinking, bewildered reaction to being showered with holy water, but at the memory of those same squinched faces as newborns, ready to let loose a howling protest at the surprise of being undressed and undiapered in the cool evening air before a bath.

But just as quickly as they blink in surprise at the sprinkling rite that celebrates Easter's new life, the boys turn to each other and chuckle at the water drops across their foreheads. As we sing songs of baptism and blessing while the priest winds his way around the church, soaking all the parishioners with his spray of holy water, I watch as young and old smile with the recognition of this simple sacred sign.

I remember those first baths we gave our boys: the sudden relaxation, the instinctual release of tiny tense limbs into warm water, the surrounding presence so familiar that the body cannot help but sink into deep memory. This is how baptism must feel – immersion into the all-surrounding love of God. This is what our Easter renewal of baptismal vows is meant to evoke: not the tired recitation of faith's facts to which we mumble our assent, but the earliest memory of a love so vast and safe around us that we relax and release into its presence and promise.

I wonder if I trust in the promise of my baptism in the same way. So often in this life of faith I wrestle with questions and ponderings and doubts that tense my limbs like a nervous newborn bracing for the bath. But watching Sam and Thomas giggle in the pew with traces of baptism dripping down their foreheads, remembering their own transformations from fear to trust, I pray once again to live into my own calling as a Christian.

With the same calm of a child held in warm water by strong hands.

PARENTING TOWARD POSSIBILITY

Do you clearly understand what you are undertaking?
Rite of Baptism

When Thomas was six weeks old, my mother and I dressed him in the long baptismal gown that four generations of my family have worn. As she did when Sam was baptised two years earlier, she told the story of how her mother had been the first to wear the garment, how her sister had to let out the neck seams for her plump babies to fit comfortably, how one niece had used OxiClean (to everyone's horror) to brighten the white, but how the gown remained unspoiled through a century of baptisms around the world.

I watched my mother's hands carefully guide Thomas's tiny arms through the linen sleeves, and I wondered where this baby's journey of faith would lead him. Would his be a straight and certain road? A dark and winding path? Or would it be a way he refused to follow at all?

I had no idea. I had only hopes.

———

The summer Thomas was born was one of the hottest on record in Minnesota.

For weeks I sweated through the sweltering heat and camped out in the cool of the basement, venturing upstairs only to refill the ice in my glass. Sam was nearly two, full of toddling energy, pressing his pudgy nose up against the steamy glass of the sliding door, begging to play outside. I sighed at every eager request, heaving my giant belly off the couch to indulge him in a rare romp in the backyard before the jungle heat overwhelmed me and I had to drag him back into the air conditioning.

I couldn't wait for the baby – and a cooler autumn – to come.

To amuse myself as the due date approached, I wrote a daily 'Dear Baby' letter to inform the child within my womb how we were waiting impatiently for his or her arrival. Sometimes the short notes were sentimental: *I know you will come in your own sweet time.* Sometimes they slid toward snarky sarcasm: *Still not here yet? Swell. Oh wait, those are my ankles.*

But the letters were always full of the wonder that waiting for a child wraps around expectant parents. Would this baby be a boy or a girl? Would he or she be healthy? What glimpses of budding personality would we see when we held our baby after birth?

As August ripened and the skin across my stomach stretched to taut, the hopeful tone in my letters began to tip toward doubt. Could we handle another child? Was our family ready for this transition? Would I be a good mother to two?

I had no idea. I had only hopes.

Then one humid night as I tossed and turned in bed, thrashing the sheets I complained were too hot for sleep, I abruptly sat up and stared at Franco.

'I think my water just broke,' I said.

'Are you sure?' he asked with surprise.

But before we could debate the question, contractions started coming quicker than I could count. While I tried to catch my breath on the couch downstairs, he called his mother to come watch Sam. Suddenly my legs started shaking, my teeth began to chatter, and an unmistakable nausea seized my contracting belly. The telltale signs of the transition stage in childbirth that signals baby's imminent arrival.

Even in the midst of labour's mental fog, I knew this unexpected, early transition was coming way too soon. Franco and I had joked about having the baby in the car en route to the hospital, but now I began to doubt that we could make the twenty-minute drive.

There was no way I was ready for this.

My mother-in-law appeared on our front step as I was inching my way to the door. Clutching Franco's arm to keep myself upright, I winced with each slow step we took toward the car. He called the hospital's birth centre as we sped through stoplights with warm night air racing in the open windows. While he consulted the nurse, I hollered through a huge contraction.

There was a pause on the phone. 'Are you sure there's no closer hospital you can get to?' I overheard the nurse ask him.

'Are you kidding me?' I wailed as we raced on.

Franco calmly coached me through fourteen miles of winding highway, and then squealed the car up to the emergency room doors, where two nurses stood waiting with a wheelchair. As they sprinted me through the hospital halls, I couldn't gasp out a single answer to their questions. And when the elevator doors opened into the birth centre, I stared into the receptionist's wide eyes as she dropped the paperwork she'd been holding. 'I guess we'll just check you in later?' she called after us as they hurried me down the hallway.

Before they had time to slap an ID bracelet on my wrist, Thomas Andrew was born.

One year after his fast and furious birth, I look down at my stocky toddler, thrashing and kicking the floor in frustration. A typical tantrum for our strong-willed Thomas.

We are in the gathering space at church, where I have exiled us to wait out the latest cranky spell until he can return to the pew in peace. For a new walker eager to practise and an almost-talker eager to be heard, Sunday Mass is nearly impossible at this stage. Franco and I take turns trading off Thomas-duty so at least one of us can be present during part of the service.

While I wait for him to work out his latest frustration on the carpet, I watch through the windows as our pastor prepares to celebrate a baptism. Standing next to the parents and godparents near the font, he asks the familiar questions I've heard hundreds of times before:

What name do you give your child?
What do you ask of God's Church for your child?
Do you clearly understand what you are undertaking?

> Rite of Baptism

Then the priest pauses and turns with a smile. 'I always laugh when I ask parents that question. As if they have any clue.'

The congregation chuckles quietly. I look down at my dark-haired boy kicking at my feet. Do I clearly understand what I am undertaking? Trying to raise him in the Church when all the headlines and surveys scream that faith is becoming more unpopular every day?

I have no idea. I have only hopes.

But deep in my bones I believe this is the most important thing I'm trying to do as a parent, to awaken my children to the possibilities of faith and a life lived for others out of love. Isn't that what all mothers and fathers do – parent toward possibility? No matter children's age or ability, no matter their stage or situation, we dream of their potential, what they might do and become.

Baptism is the same. We are welcomed into a community that has great hopes for us. We are called by God who dreams of all that we might become. But this first sacrament also celebrates the simple fact of being beloved. Of knowing that we do not need to achieve to be worthy or succeed to be faithful. My hopes for my children and their faith hang between this tension: I hope it will inspire them to do and remind them to be.

I watch as the priest dips his hand into the bubbling water and the parents lean over the font, holding their baby wearing a long white gown, just like the one that my babies wore, that my siblings and cousins and aunts and uncles wore, with the hopes and dreams of our families wrapped around us in the clean white promise of what our new life might become.

As Thomas kicks at my ankles, I think back to the night before his baptism when I wrote him another letter, this time of the hopes I had for him: that he would not take his baptism lightly, that he would spend a lifetime growing into what it means to be loved by God. The simplest summary of my answers to the same questions our pastor was posing to new parents today: what I ask of God's Church for my child and what I believe about what I am undertaking. All the challenges I will face as his mother – from toddler tantrums to teenage rebellions – will be wrapped up in these same hopes of faith, just as they were bound up in the story of his baptism and the story of his birth.

When I lay shaking and quivering on the basement couch the night Thomas was born, overwhelmed by a labour that was coming too fast and too hard, I learned all over again that as a parent, I am never fully ready for the transformations I am called to face. I may never clearly know what I am undertaking. But I do know this: that life is made up of the leaps we take toward what God desires for us. Leaps of faith as we plunge into the unknown, gathering our hopes around us.

Trying once again to trust toward possibility.

CHAPTER TWO

Celebrating Grace – Confirmation

INFERTILITY'S LONG INITIATION

*Now hope that is seen is not hope. For who hopes for
what is seen? But if we hope for what we do not see,
we wait for it with patience.*
*Likewise the Spirit helps us in our weakness; for we do
not know how to pray as we ought, but that very
Spirit intercedes with sighs too deep for words.*

Romans 8:24–6

The first few weeks felt thrilling. Here we go, taking the leap!
We could have a baby any time! We'd only been married a year
and I was still in grad school, but this yearning tugged at our
hearts and wouldn't let go. We'd prayed about the decision
and trusted that it felt right to try right now. We'd make it
work. After all, this was everything we'd ever wanted: a baby
to make our lives complete.

Do you see where this story is headed?

Months passed. Nothing happened. Hope faltered a
few steps. Work and school were grateful distractions but
we started to worry more than wonder. It was too early to
diagnose but our instincts said something was wrong. We kept
waiting.

*Maybe you're wondering why we never saw infertility
coming.*

One year passed. We went from one book to the next,
from one doctor to the next, from one natural family planning
method to the next. None of the nexts seemed to help. My

cycle seemed stubbornly stuck on pause, unable to ovulate. I sat quietly through baby showers for other women with my own womb empty, save for the ache. My once-familiar body felt like a foreign country. We kept waiting.

'Just relax,' you want to reassure us. 'It'll happen when you least expect it.'

But once infertility enters the equation, serendipity and sexiness get sucked out of baby-making. We carefully charted every try and methodically monitored every test. We became experts at identifying the subtle phases of the female cycle. We read up on homeopathic remedies to increase fertility. I changed diets, specialists, supplements, even the window shades in our bedroom when we read that light impacts ovulation.

Now you see that we were serious.

Infertility proved one tough initiation into the prospect of parenthood.

You I know the end of the story. There were babies, obviously. So allow me to back up.

When I was fourteen, freckle-faced and frizzy-haired, I got confirmed with the rest of my eighth-grade class. Standard stuff for our small-town Catholic school: a springtime rite of passage that walked hand in hand with junior high graduation in June. I remember our religion teacher bubbling about how confirmation meant becoming an adult in the Church, and I remember picking out a flowered dress with matching cream shoes. But no one ever explained to me how memorising the seven gifts of the Spirit or scribbling a stack of service-hour slips was supposed to help me become a grown-up.

That was what high school was for, I figured, pouring over my sister's old copies of *Seventeen* magazine and trying out new drugstore lipstick in the bathroom mirror. The next four years were bound to turn me into someone mature and confident, if I could only survive freshman gym class.

Only years later did I start to realise what confirmation means: that God blesses our becoming. That what begins in baptism is affirmed as we grow into the gifts we are given. That we enter fully into our community when we claim our faith as our own. That when we echo the promises made for us in baptism and choose a new name to embrace our faith, the Church celebrates our final step toward full initiation as the bishop anoints our forehead with chrism, the sacred oil that marks the seal of the Spirit.

But what does all this have to do with infertility?

When Franco and I were knee-deep in blood draws and hormone prescriptions and doctor's appointments and ultrasounds, we never would have called the experience holy. Infertility tasted as bitter as the cold metal thermometer I slid under my tongue every morning for months, hoping in vain that my temperature would rise. Franco kept our prayers positive, but as months passed, his eyes began to flicker with doubt, too. Pregnant women and parents strolling with babies filled the shops we browsed and the streets we walked. I grew tired of the squeeze he'd give my hand when he saw me staring at yet another proud, round belly bursting with life.

But the truth I hate to admit, now on the greener side of infertility's fence, is that I never felt closer to God.

All those nights I cried myself to sleep, all those holidays that passed without a baby in our arms, all those mornings I got furious at the monitors and charts that taunted me with their lack of progress – I felt as if God were listening right on the other side of the door I'd leaned my head against in grief. I don't know why this assurance came to me in the midst of my fear and fury, but there it was. Grace. While we were being initiated into all that parenthood would mean – sacrifice, surrender and stamina for the long haul – God was present during the long process of our becoming. That presence was confirmation that we would always be companioned, even when the calling proved harder than we hoped.

Infertility forced us to rethink and reclaim everything we believed. When friends from college called to announce their good news and I dug my nails into my palms to keep from crying, I had to remember that joy was not locked away for the lucky few. When the hormone treatments made me dizzy and depressed and drove Franco crazy with my unpredictable mood swings, we both slammed up against the realisation that living into a calling can be soul-wrenching work. When I breathed in our newborn nephew's earthy scent when we met him at the hospital, I had to remind myself that God still loved us, even if we never had a baby of our own.

Perhaps infertility was the perfect initiation into the unpredictability of parenting.

You might think the story ends like this:

One cold morning in early December, I shivered in my bathrobe as I watched two faint lines appear for the first time on the pregnancy test sitting on the bathroom counter. I threw open the door and found Franco waiting impatiently in the hallway. 'Well?' he asked.

'I can't believe it!' I yelled. 'I can't believe this is really happening!'

I ran downstairs, shoved on my boots, threw on a winter coat over my pyjamas, and dragged Franco to the car so we could drive to buy more tests at the drugstore to double-check. Our tires spinning through the snowy street left two long lines on the white-covered road behind us, a deep trail in the dark through which we'd come.

Or maybe you think the story should end like this:

Eight months after that winter morning, I stared stupidly at the triage nurse who informed us that my water had indeed broken three weeks early and I would not be going home without a baby in my arms. At 8:07 the next evening I delivered our wailing 6-pound, 5-ounce son in room 242 of Mercy Hospital – a fitting name for a place where we were flooded with wonder. All three of us.

But in fact the story ends like this:

We are still becoming parents. Still being slowly initiated every day.

Parenthood in these early years – perhaps always – feels like an endless rite of passage. We are constantly pulled away from the place we think we know (babies!) and thrust into a foreign country (toddlers?). We have to regain our bearings to keep going, because as soon as we settle into the strange new world around us, we glimpse yet another unknown horizon looming ahead (preschool!). Quicker than we realise, we will have passed through the land of childhood and will be standing with our sons as they each take their confirmation vows.

When the bishop smeared sweet-smelling confirmation chrism on my forehead, I was still an awkward eighth-grader on the cusp of adolescence. I didn't know what it would mean to embrace an adult identity as a Christian. And when the nurse placed the wriggling, slimy newborn in my arms, I was still a bewildered young adult on the brink of motherhood. I didn't understand what it would mean to live into the calling of parenting. Perhaps the nature of being a novice means we can never fully understand what we embrace by our initiation when it happens. We can only try to trust in what might be revealed as we enter into the new world stretching out before us.

Because initiation is only the beginning. We are always on our way to becoming.

A STRONG HAND ON THE SHOULDER

As a rule there should be a sponsor for each of those to be confirmed. These sponsors bring the candidates to receive the sacrament, present them to the minister for the anointing, and will later help them to fulfil their baptismal promises faithfully under the influence of the Holy Spirit whom they have received.

Introduction to Rite of Confirmation

When the time came to get confirmed, I was a nervous wreck. A frazzled teenager with fraying nerves. I'd lie on my bed, sprawled across my pink comforter, staring up at the glow-in-the-dark stars stuck across my ceiling, and I'd obsess about all that could go wrong.

I was worried about picking a confirmation name. Should I keep my familiar old middle name? Choose something new and grown-up? Was I supposed to pick the name of a favourite saint, and what happened if I didn't have a favourite – was I not a good Catholic? Could I even get confirmed?

I was petrified about meeting the bishop. What if he was grouchy and glared at me over his glasses? What if he quizzed me on Church doctrine and I choked? What if I dropped the notecard with my rote responses to the ritual's questions, and it got trampled under the feet of my classmates waiting behind me, and then I showed up at the front of the church empty-handed and clueless?

I was even anxious about getting blessed with the chrism. What if the oil made my pimpled forehead even shinier in the pictures my mom would snap? What if it messed up my hair? Could I wash it off before the reception in the church hall or would the sacrament not stick? (Clearly confirmation was a trigger for teenage neuroses.)

The only part that didn't freak me out was picking a sponsor. For that choice I didn't have to think twice.

My Aunt Sarah was my youngest aunt, closest to me in age. She made mix tapes for me and took me to my first Jimmy Buffet concert and let me sleep over at her condo with plush white carpeting. She cracked funny jokes and drove a convertible and painted her fingernails bright red. But she also went to church on Sundays and worked at our local Catholic high school as a football trainer, making her – in my mind – the ideal confirmation sponsor: both cool and Catholic. What more could a girl want?

Still I was terrified to call her up and ask her to be my sponsor. While her number rang, I twisted the spiral phone cord around my finger till it turned purple. But she piped an enthusiastic 'Sure!' to my request, and I gave a sigh of relief. With my aunt standing behind me, her hand strong on my shoulder, I would not faint from fear or crumble at the bishop's feet or look like a total loser in the class photos.

(I hoped, anyway.)

Fast-forward fourteen years. While I had freaked out about plenty of things in the past – tennis team trials and homecoming dance dates, calculus finals and college applications, freshman orientation and study abroad, first dates and bad breakups, job searches and cross-country moves, wedding planning and grad school papers – nothing terrified me half as much as the prospect of giving birth.

I have always been a notorious wimp when it comes to pain, known to wince at the slightest shove from my younger brothers and nurse a paper cut for hours. So when it came to childbirth I was scared stiff. As much as I always wanted to be a mother, I had secretly hoped that researchers would discover a pain-free labour process by the time I had to deliver. But such miracles continue to elude the medical profession, as evidenced by veteran moms' battle stories.

'I pushed for eight straight hours,' bragged one woman at a baby shower I attended while pregnant. 'That's nothing,' scoffed another who shared our sofa. 'I was in labour for four solid days. I thought I was going to die.'

I slunk off to refill my punch cup.

At the childbirth classes Franco and I attended, my knees started to wobble as soon as I saw the pictographs on the 'Pain Scale Chart' plastered on the hospital wall: early labour's yellow smiley face, active labour's clenched orange cheeks, transition's sweaty red brow, and delivery's tortured purple grimace – puffing, panting, and panic-stricken.

No cartoon should look like that, I thought. And *my* face should certainly never look like that.

I started to sink down slowly in my seat while the nurse pushed play on the childbirth video. Franco's elbow nudged my side. 'You OK?' he asked, raising an eyebrow.

Am I OK? I thought. *I have a giant creature growing in my belly that I have to birth into this world through a Pain Scale torment that will contort my face into a screaming scarlet cartoon of exploding pain, and you're asking if I'm OK?*

'I'm fine,' I lied, patting his hand.

As the delivery date neared, I knew I needed help. I started emailing friends who'd had babies, began peppering family members with questions, and practically attacked any woman in the diaper aisle for advice. Their patient encouragement – *you can do it, you are strong, millions of women have gone before you* – would help for a while, but eventually anxiety grabbed hold again, wearying me with worry.

Until one afternoon toward the end of the third trimester when I plopped down in the new glider in the nursery, freshly painted by my mother and mother-in-law, who had spent an afternoon laughing together as they covered the walls with sky blue. I closed my eyes and pushed back gently to rock, tired but trying to pray through my birth fears. After a few quiet minutes I felt the strangest sense that my grandmothers were standing next to me, one on my left and one on my right. Silent and smiling, strong and loving.

My eyes flew open with a rush of reassurance. I sat blinking in the sunlight streaming through the bedroom window. Why had my grandmas come to mind? Both had died years earlier; they rarely crossed my daily thoughts. But I couldn't shake the familiar warmth of their soft, wrinkled hands resting on my shoulders. Were they sending support for the labour I feared, the labour they each knew so well, with thirteen babies between them?

From that moment on, I started to see small signs of strong women all around me. I folded laundry full of comfy maternity clothes shared by my sister. I hung up a tiny blue and purple sweater in the baby's closet, hand-knit by my aunt. I read the parenting book on my nightstand that my sister-in-law had given me. I filled the nursery's bookshelves with childhood classics from friends who'd picked out their favourites as baby shower presents.

I began to realise that I was never alone, that strong hands were on my shoulders no matter where I went.

When my water broke early and labour loomed quickly, the labour I'd been dreading for months, the same women rallied round me. My mom and sister called throughout the hours to send their love, texting encouragement and hoping for updates. My gentle friend Katie served as our doula in the delivery room, coaching me through contractions and fetching cups of ice chips. My friends from grad school dug out the candles I'd asked them to light when they got the news that I was in labour. Outside the walls of the hospital, even halfway across the world, the women in my life prayed me through my fears.

I had never phoned a single one of them to ask if she'd be my sponsor, if she'd mentor me into mothering. But bearing down under the bright lights of the delivery room, I ended up with a whole circle of women holding me steady by the shoulders.

What I learned when I was twenty-eight, smiling bewilderedly in the photos as Franco and I cradled our newborn baby, is what I missed when I was fourteen, grinning for the camera next to my aunt on the church steps. Being confirmed is not only about the individual who is initiated, but also the community that welcomes its newest member, spilling over with joy at adding one more and promising support for the struggles that lie ahead. In the same way, all the women who were with me in labour, in spirit or in person – mothers, grandmothers, aunts, sisters, and friends – they were the hands resting reassuringly on my shoulder, the feet standing firm behind me.

Their wisdom was the strength that bore me through.

THE SPIRIT'S FLASHES

When you search for me, you will find me;
if you seek me with all your heart, I will let you find me,
   says the Lord ...
            Jeremiah 29:13–14

Wet crib sheets at morning light. Forks clattering to the floor at breakfast. Timeouts for slapping over sharing trains. Tears over torn pages from dog-eared books. Teething tantrums and runny noses. Potty training accidents and three changes of clothes. Scraped elbows at the playground and meltdowns at the grocery checkout. Nap ending too early; dinner starting too late; bedtime dragging out way too long.

When the final requests for one more story and a second glass of water and an extra snuggle and another trip to the bathroom have all been answered, and the last bedroom door clicks shut behind me, I let out the exhale I've been holding for hours. Finally. It's over.

So many days of parenting little ones are like this. Endless. Exhausting. Exasperating.

By evening's end I feel my skin crawling with the desire to collapse on the couch with a glass of wine and wave the white flag of defeat. Inevitably these are the same days when a grandmotherly stranger in the shop smiles at the chaos erupting from my shopping cart and clucks a kindly cliché about *enjoying every minute because they grow up so fast.* I grit my teeth and try to thank her, screaming a silent protest in my head that *I will never, ever miss right now.*

Yet without fail, the maddening days are also the ones when a tiny gem of a moment – a baby who smiles for the first time in the middle of bedtime bedlam, a toddler who blesses my door-slammed finger with a sloppy kiss, or a boy who throws his arms around his brother's neck in an unprompted hug – peels back the scales from my eyes. I catch my breath in wonder at how good this parenting work can be, how full of astonishing beauty and joy. My own clichés scramble to capture the truth already fleeting before my eyes – that God is here, that this is holy, that all is grace.

But even when the crystalline moment evaporates as wails erupt from the next room, I know that something of the Spirit has surfaced here. And if I keep my eyes open, I might start to see more.

———

Grace is surprising by definition. We do not earn it, we cannot control it, we will not tame it. But if we notice when it emerges and trust in its promise, then the whole tenor of the room around us starts to shift. We become witnesses to the slow, small work of the Spirit.

Sometimes I still slip into the temptation of thinking that time with God should be like gazing onto a serene morning lake, a smooth mirror reflecting the wide blue sky above, a quiet shore where I sit basking in rays of rising sun. I crave these moments of calm when children are hurling themselves into my knees while I dig in the fridge for leftovers to reheat for dinner. I start to idealise – even idolise – the silence and stillness that should radiate as proof of God's peace, if I could only shush the constant chatter in the cluttered kitchen around me.

But the creation story says the Spirit hovered over the chaos of the waters, close to the murky mess. And if I'm honest, even as I indulge in late-afternoon daydreams about escaping to the lake to meditate, this God-in-chaos is the God I meet more often.

The God who settles over the living room litter of broken crayons and skittering Matchbox cars and crushed Cheerios underfoot.

The God who waits in the middle of our messy mudroom as we scramble out the door for school, feet crammed in shoes and arms stuffed in jackets and back-packs flung over shoulders.

The God who hovers above the fragile hour before dinner, when tempers are flaring fast and hot like oven burners sparked to boil.

The God who reminds a frazzled mother, patiently and persistently, that there is no need to escape when all the love she needs to learn is right at her feet.

Because the gifts of the Spirit that I had to memorise as an eighth-grader preparing for the sacrament – wonder and wisdom, reverence and right judgement, knowledge and courage and understanding – were never confined to a moment's confirmation. They were promised for the whole of life. Even the days flooded with leaky diapers and broken basement pipes and a full gallon of milk dumped across the counter by a boy who was only trying to help.

One late summer evening, Sam and I linger outside as the last streaks of sun spill purple across the sky, the first stars twinkling faint through thin clouds. His hair is damp, clinging to the back of his neck, and his cheeks are still flushed from the bath. His feet dance across the deck, a last burst of excitement at this unexpected break from the bedtime routine. When I spy the first flash of eerie neon light – 'Look! By the trees!' – he races over and presses his nose through the railing's wooden slats.

Together we scan the lawn for lightning bugs, waiting impatiently for more to appear. And they do – abruptly, unbidden, flickering past us through the dusk. As I stare at one to track its steady flashing across the yard, I catch glimpses of other tiny flitting lights, too. Did a whole swarm emerge from the darkness of the woods beyond? Or were they hiding right near us all along and my eyes hadn't yet adjusted to see? Either way we marvel at them together – 'Mama, there's more!' – awed by their otherness, their ability to make light, to be light, to find their way through the night.

Fireflies, lightning bugs – their names are misnomers, I muse while Sam counts the insects gathering at the wood's edge. Theirs is not a bonfire's blaze smoking in the evening air, nor stormy strikes brightening the sky overhead. And neither 'fly' nor 'bug' captures the elegance of their silent flashes, a summer night's rare gift. But when Sam smiles up at me, his blue eyes bright in the settling dark, I remember how words falter in luminous moments.

I ruffle his thick blonde hair and tell him five more minutes till we need to scoot to bed. But I crouch down beside him in the gathering dusk and peer through the wooden slats where he watches. We wait a little longer, lingering in the night world awakening around us as crickets and frogs tune their throaty song.

Perhaps God, too, is best glimpsed in the darkness, where our eyes narrow to pierce the shadows and our hearts leap to the sight of light, no matter how slender. Deep within me hums an assurance that we have not seen the last. Grace will be there, again and always, quiet and unassuming, no matter how fleeting it flashes in the moment. Tomorrow will bring another glimmer, if only I keep my eyes open wide enough to see the beauty behind the ordinary.

Sam shivers and presses his small back against my legs, his pyjamas summer thin in the cooling air. Reluctantly we head back inside. As I tug the sheets up to his chin while he burrows into bed, I see his eyes still sparling in the dark of his room. 'Amazing, Mama,' he whispers as I kiss his head.

Yawning, I pad down the hallway to our bedroom. But before I zip down the window blinds, I pause and peek out once more. Fireflies still flit at the yard's edge, now edging toward our neighbours' trees. I settle into sleep easier somehow, knowing they are still there.

They are commonplace confirmations, these everyday encounters with the Spirit. The pauses of presence when we are renewed with peace. The unexpected flashes of joy that pulse with God's bright love. The dark nights, even after long days, when we turn to sleep with fireflies still flickering behind our eyes.

Part II
RHYTHMS: EUCHARIST, RECONCILIATION, AND ANOINTING OF THE SICK

Rhythms mark the time. Life with little ones hums along to a beat all its own. Early morning wake-ups and midnight cries. Three meals a day and snacks on the side. Nap time and playtime. Bath time and bedtime. From the earliest days a family follows this most basic tempo – the cadences of childhood.

Rhythms set the pace. Sacraments have their own rhythms that beckon us back. Take and eat. Repent and forgive. Bless and heal. The three sacraments that respond to our most basic needs – for food, forgiveness, and healing – are repeatable: Eucharist, reconciliation, and anointing of the sick. Catholics can receive Communion daily, confess to a priest whenever needed and seek anointing with sacred oil when a serious sickness arises, not just for death's last rites. These sacramental repetitions remind us how God never fails to meet us in our humanity.

EVERYDAY SACRAMENT

Rhythms keep us moving. Each day in our house we return to these three practices, too. We gather around the table and give thanks. We ask forgiveness after fights. We help heal with words of comfort. Our domestic practices of Eucharist, reconciliation and anointing shape who we become. Everyday sacraments set the pulse for our family's life together.

Rhythms draw us together. The repeatability of these rhythms is humbling. We all need to eat, to be forgiven and to be healed. Children, dependent on adults for food, care, and comfort, remind us daily of this truth. We cannot live beyond our body and our nature. These universal experiences affirm the sacred nature of breaking bread together, forgiving as we have been forgiven and seeking God's healing power.

Rhythms keep repeating. This is why a sacramental view of parenting makes sense. Every day we live into these movements of nourishing and nurturing, loving and letting go, tending and helping to heal. We practise the rhythms that remind us how God, like a loving parent, cares for us and gives us what we need.

CHAPTER THREE

Broken for You – Eucharist

THIS IS MY BODY, GIVEN FOR YOU

> *When the hour came, he took his place at the table, and*
> *the apostles with him ... Then he took a loaf of bread,*
> *and when he had given thanks, he broke it and gave*
> *it to them, saying, 'This is my body, which is given for*
> *you. Do this in remembrance of me.'*
>
> Luke 22:14, 19

You are a whisper of a whirl curled up deep in my belly. The hormonal soup in which you swim makes me nauseous at all hours of the day. I choke down crackers when I wake, throw up in the sink before breakfast, and pull over at gas stations to get sick on the drive to work. I collapse on the couch before sunset most evenings, too tired to drag myself to bed.

I am three months pregnant. This is my body, given for you.

You are growing as fast as my waistline. My stomach swells into stretchy maternity shirts as your limbs flip within me. Food tastes good again, but everything I eat gives me heartburn. Strangers ask when I am due; they raise their eyebrows when they hear how much longer we have to go. I toss and turn all night, trying to find a comfortable position for sleep. I can no longer see my feet.

I am six months pregnant. This is my body, given for you.

Your feet jab my ribs; your knees nudge my sides; your elbows trace strange trails across my skin. My belly has pushed far past the point of comfort; every elastic waist- band slides down the basketball of my stomach. My taut skin itches constantly, my ankles swell from the weight they carry, and my back aches a new twinge each morning. I tire from a walk around the block. Contractions have been coming for weeks, but no progress. People stare wide-eyed when I promise you're not twins.

I am nine months pregnant. This is my body, given for you.

You come fast, before the epidural has time to kick in. The pain breaks me open: there is so much blood I think it might be death but everyone in the room tells me this is life. You arrive in a rush and they pull you out and into my arms as I gasp for air; they worry about your breathing and whisk you away while my empty body longs for you. I let strangers stitch me up and wash me off and help me dress; then I lean on your father's arms to limp down the hall to the nursery. When they finally let me hold you, I fear my heart might thump out of my chest. I am sore and scarred, but nothing hurts as badly as when we have to leave you at night and drive home with the car seat still empty in the back.

I am three days postpartum. This is my body, given for you.

You are nestled into home now, safe and sound. You grow ounces and inches every week, fluttering open your dark blue eyes to soak up this strange new world. You sleep in spurts and wake wailing in the night, desperate for milk and mama. I drag myself to sitting and pull you into my tired arms as my head throbs and my eyelids droop. I fear I will never sleep again. I am learning to nurse, painfully slow, through swollen soreness and lousy latches. My stomach is spongy as it shrinks, and my hair is thinning faster than my weight trudging back down the scale. But every day I catch my breath at how perfect you become. I barely remember a time when you were not.

I am six weeks postpartum. This is my body, given for you.

You doze in the car seat while I lean on the pew's edge, too exhausted to kneel up straight. I stare at the altar, trying to pray through a sleepy fog while the priest intones the words I've heard a thousand times before. Bread becomes body, wine becomes blood. For the first time I ache into what sacrifice means, what it means to be bread and blood for others. We are broken open so that love might take life within us. You start to fuss, and instinctively my hands reach out to pull you to me.

I am your mother. This is my body, given for you.

LESSONS FROM THE DINNER TABLE

Do this in memory of me. The mystery of faith.

Eucharistic Prayer of the Mass

We spill in the door from Sunday Mass, hungry for lunch. Both boys are whining, the dog is dancing around my feet, and I'm mentally running through the fridge's contents before I reach the kitchen. Spiritual nourishment is fine, but this family needs to eat.

We pull stacks of Tupperware from the fridge and scoop out last night's leftovers onto four dishes. Sam won't eat potatoes; Thomas won't touch corn. One wants milk, one cries for water. Their protests at washing hands are interrupted only by microwave beeps pestering that plates need to be switched. In my last dizzy spin around the counter while they're clamouring to eat, I grab forks, spoons, napkins, four glasses, one bib, and a sippy cup; I plop everything at the table, myself in a chair, and look up at the grimaced faces waiting for grace.

Just another meal in paradise.

After we hold hands to sing thanks, I start to scarf down my food before its warmth evaporates with the predictable request to accompany someone to the potty. While I chew I think back to quieter moments during Communion an hour earlier. Such humble bread compared to the spread before me: merely a mouthful at Mass, not a meal to savour. And a small sip of wine that's shared, not a generous glass to enjoy on my own. But Eucharist is the only sacrament I can swallow. It is the only truth I can taste.

Today's turn through the communion line was typical Sunday chaos: Sam wandered away while I cupped my hands to receive the bread; Thomas tried to grab the chalice when I reached out to take the wine. Reverence is too much to ask of toddlers, and I can't blame them for being oblivious to the moment's meaning.

But as I rise from the table to grab seconds for my hungry eaters, I realise that right here is where they are learning to take and eat, to bless and share. Here is where we practise communion: giving thanks, breaking bread, feeding the hungry. Here is where we teach and forgive and celebrate and praise. Here is where we love in flesh and blood.

It's a messy love, smeared across chins and hands and high chairs, sometimes spilled or spit up or snubbed in protest. But it's a faithful love, a promise of plenty. Being a parent means I will do everything I can to give my kids good food to fill their stomachs as long as they're under my roof. God must feel the same when we gather as a hungry church, starving to become more like the Christ we try to follow.

Too often I overlook the importance of our family table. Mealtime becomes another chore: the everyday work of preparing dinner while cajoling cranky children, the frenzied flurry of serving and supervising the meal, the chaos of cleaning up and coaxing tired kids to head upstairs for bath and bed.

By my estimations we have shared over four thousand meals at this table since our children started eating solid food. At least half of those meals have involved tears over spilled drinks, battles over vegetables, and prolonged parental negotiations over one-last-bite. It's an exhausting labour of love to keep everyone well fed. I know family dinners are important, but most nights I collapse into a chair after the dishes are washed, food put away, floor swept, and counters wiped clean. I'm too tired to think about the deeper meaning of what we do at this simple wooden table – the sacredness of meeting each other over meals. Eucharist can be like this, too. I can breeze through Communion, worried about keeping my kids in line and forgetting the wonder of encountering God in such an intimate way. I love this sacrament deep in my bones; it challenges and comforts me; its truth and transformation keep me Catholic. But the distractions of my life can domesticate the power of Eucharist if I'm not careful. If I let the ordinary elements of bread and wine stay ordinary. *Do this in memory of me*, Christ said. For years I thought this meant *come to church, pray the prayers, eat the bread and drink the wine.* Only when I had to make a home and set a table for my family did I understand what he really meant.

Do everything in memory of me.

Feed the hungry at your own table in memory of me.

Welcome the children and invite the strangers and break open your blessings and pour yourself out in memory of me.

Do everything in memory of me.

It becomes an everyday Eucharist, our three square meals round this humble circle. If I squint with eyes of faith, the same faith that believes bread and wine can become Christ among us, I see how good this time at the table is for each of us – we who serve and we who receive. The real presence of Christ is right here, too.

But the sight of Thomas throwing sweet potato chunks to the dog snaps me back from my reverie. No time to theologise once the food starts flying. I smile at Sam giggling at his brother, but next thing I know he's slipped off his chair and is wailing for a kiss to make the bumped knee all better. Crying being contagious, Thomas starts to bawl out of sympathy.

'I think that about wraps up lunch,' Franco sighs as he scoots back his chair to grab a washcloth and swab Thomas's sweet-potatoed face.

Just another meal in paradise, we laugh.

Do this in memory of me.

CHRYSALIS IN THE COMMUNION LINE

If you are the body and members of Christ,
then it is your sacrament that is placed on the table of
the Lord; it is your sacrament that you receive.

St Augustine, Sermon 272, quoted in *Catechism of
the Catholic Church*, 1396

During his first month of preschool, Sam brought home a craft
showing the butterfly's life cycle. On construction paper he
had glued four pieces of dry pasta: a tiny seed of orzo for the
egg, a corkscrew-shaped rotini for the caterpillar, a shell for
the chrysalis, and a bowtie for the butterfly. When prodded
he offered the names of each stage, but 'chrysalis' was his
favourite.

We laughed to hear the elegant word tripping off a three-
year-old's lisping tongue. But the small shell curved in on
itself, a tiny curl of protection, waiting in silence to become
the butterfly tucked inside, was a perfect image for his tender
age. Preschool was a push for our cautious Sam, the one born
with wide wondering eyes that always seemed stunned at the
world whirling around him. It took weeks of wailing at drop-
off before he accepted the transition. A small step toward
becoming a big kid.

I watched Sam sitting quietly at the kitchen table, slowly
turning up each flap on the paper to find what lay hidden
underneath. His eyes met mine as he gave a small smile.
'Chrysalis,' he whispered. I saw him inside that shell, growing
gently inside his earliest years of childhood, transforming in
ways we could not glimpse from the outside.

Was I tucked into my own shell, too? Was this why
becoming a mother sometimes felt so dark and slow, a long
transformation into new life?

When Sam was a few months old, I took him to a baby class at our local community centre. In the classroom lined with colourful toys and stacks of blocks, pairs of mothers and infants circled around a big blanket and cooed at each other while waiting for class to begin. Then the teacher asked us to start by sharing one thing that had surprised us about becoming a parent.

How would I pick just one? Everything about my life felt completely different. What I ate, what I wore, when I slept, where I went – all of it had been transformed by the arrival of tiny Sam. But the most bewildering part was how long it was taking to adjust to this transition. I kept wishing for peace, for clarity, for comfort in the midst of all the upheaval. Shouldn't I start feeling like a mother already?

Lost in my thoughts, I was startled to hear a cheerful voice pipe up next to me: 'I guess I'm just surprised by how easy it's been!'

I turned my head slowly to stare, feeling like I'd been swept into the Wild West movie scene where the saloon music skids to a stop as everyone looks up to see the stranger who's just pushed through the still-swinging double doors. Was she serious?

She was. Her baby slept like a dream, she said, and nursed like a champ. She was just so happy; her husband, too. Everything was easier than she expected.

Run away now, a voice inside my head screamed to me. *You don't belong here!* But as I looked around at the circle of mothers who looked as tired and trying-to-be-cheerful as I was, I hoped I wasn't the only one who felt shocked into silence.

Eventually one brave woman broke the hush by quietly confessing that colic was making her crazy. Another started crying as she talked about going back to work and leaving her baby. I finally offered that I was overwhelmed by how hard nursing had been – I thought it was supposed to be simple. As each mom spoke, heads started to nod sympathetically.

But when class ended and I picked up my overstuffed diaper bag to leave, it was the first mother's declaration of easy joy that crawled under my skin and clung to me as I strapped Sam back in his car seat. What was I doing wrong? How was this so hard?

Why was it taking me so long to feel like a mother?

Back when I was a new mom, my 3 a.m. prayers were full of pleas to God to help me parent in a way worthy of the child I had received. How I longed to burst into full confidence and take off flying, to face the world as a mother who knew what she was doing. But I wanted more than my hands could hold. I wanted to become a self-assured, seasoned expert overnight. Instead I had to slog through the transition like all parents before me whose babies prompted their becoming new.

Turns out that Communion would save me during that newborn stage. Not only the afternoons I began to spend in solidarity with other mothers whose friendship I devoured, but the flutter of a pause each Sunday at Mass when, for an instant, I ceased to be solely the source of nourishment for a needy newborn and could be fed myself. I would come forward and reach out my hands like a child hungry for bread and drink deeply of the cup I was given. And when I sank back into my seat, I felt a flicker of something that was not confidence or cool collectedness, but calm. A simple peace. The hope of what I might become.

EVERYDAY SACRAMENT

What I didn't understand the day when I envied another mother's ease is how becoming a parent takes time. The first stage started when a spark took shape inside me: a tiny egg trembling with new life. The second stage began when I birthed my baby and the two of us crawled out into the world like caterpillars trying out new limbs. But it was the third stage – this chrysalis phase of feeling trapped in a dark shell, confined by the cocoon around me – that felt endless in the early years of parenting. For so long I felt flipped upside down, hanging by a thread to whatever branch held me.

Now I start to sense how it takes a lifetime. This gift of a child that we receive with shaking hands turns us slowly into parents, a transformation we cannot control.

———

Every Sunday at church I watch children as they walk up for Communion. Some stare wide-eyed at each pew they pass. Others wander obliviously. The smallest ones totter alongside their parents, bumping into strangers' legs. Older ones drag their feet and have to be prodded along to keep the line moving. I see the babies squirm and the big kids race to catch up, and I wonder how they look to God who waits to welcome each of us.

Each child in the communion line is a chrysalis: the newborn nestled on her father's shoulder, the toddler kicking to be set free from his mother's arms, the preschooler pulling her sister's pigtails, the grade-schooler growing impatient behind his grandma's walker, the teenager slinking back to her seat before someone sees. Each one is in the midst of becoming something – someone – new. But it is a transformation so steady and slow we can miss it unfolding before our eyes.

Sometimes I want to rush my kids along, nudge them to grow up a little faster, to wipe their own bottoms or tie their own shoes or make their own lunch. But I can't pry them out of their shells before their time. It is not magic that brings wisdom and maturity: it is patient, plodding growth.

Do we, their parents, remember this truth: that we are always becoming? With all the words we use to describe Eucharist – precious, sacred, holy – do we dare to see ourselves as beloved in God's eyes, too? Each Sunday's turn down the aisle toward the altar reminds me how Communion is a sacrament of already and not-yet. We receive as we are, and we become what we receive.

Each time I shuffle toward the front of the line to the stranger who will offer me the sacrament, I wonder how to trust that I am gradually becoming the person and parent God invites me to be. Waiting in the dark of the chrysalis takes time, a long and slow stretch of patient time. But like the antsy children I see at church, like that anxious mother I was in the new baby class, I am on the way, too. The way toward becoming something I cannot yet see.

CHAPTER FOUR

From Frustration to Forgiveness – Reconciliation

WHEN HE LOVED THE SITTER MORE THAN ME

Forgive, and you will be forgiven; give and it will be given to you. A good measure, pressed down, shaken together, running over, will be put into your lap; for the measure you give will be the measure you get back.

Luke 6:37–8

'No, Mama! I don't want you! I want Samantha!'

Sam sits straight up in his tiny toddler bed, surrounded by stuffed animals as he sobs for the babysitter. 'I don't want you to be here! I only want Samantha!'

Every cell in my body quivers, screaming out against this rejection of my very self. Doesn't he know it's me he's supposed to love, supposed to call for, supposed to cling to above any other? Doesn't he know what it means that I'm his mother?

I try to remind myself that he's only three years old, trying to figure out a confusing world of adults and work schedules and who's in charge. All he knows is that the sitter put him to bed last night, so she should be here when he awakes. And now what I'd envisioned as a lovely morning of cuddling with my boys, pancakes for breakfast and pyjamas till noon, is crumbling under his unexpected greeting.

I sink to my knees next to his bed, stretch out my arms to pull him into my lap, shaking inside as I try to breathe. I want to be understanding and patient and not start crying myself or – even worse – explode in anger at how deeply his words cut me.

But he pushes my arms away in protest, hot tears streaming down his flushed cheeks.

'No, Mama!' he wails even louder. 'I don't want you!'

———~~~———

All morning I nurse my hurt, steaming over a cup of hot tea, brooding in the kitchen as my boys play in the living room. I serve breakfast with a small smile and kiss each mop of hair as they devour their pancakes. But I can't shake the feeling that I've failed, that I'm not a good enough mother.

As they scamper off to the land of Duplos and dinosaur books, I sit down to try to make sense of my muddled morning.

First I try to rationalise. Surely this latest round of rejection in favour of the childcare help I've hired is not an indictment of my parenting or the loss of my cherished place in my son's life.

But logic is weak when I'm a wreck.

Then I try to sermonise. Maybe Sam's momentary rejection of me as a mother is symbolic of my own rejections of God, my selfish protests that shove away the offer of love that created and sustains me.

But theologising is tough when I feel like crap.

Because my boy has been doing this for weeks, crying when I come to get him in the morning and not Franco or the sitter, ignoring my gentle lessons to 'use kind words'. Even my best efforts to keep my chin up and remember that 'it's just a phase' are starting to fall flat.

Frankly, I'm angry. I know it's unfair: he's a wee three years old and he never means to hurt me. He's simply being honest and emotional and exactly his age.

But his words strike the most vulnerable spot. It's the unspoken fear of every mother who hires help to care for her children – that one day my baby will love the other woman more than me. Irrational, insecure, but an unavoidable fear. So I still have to forgive him this unintentional wound.

I sigh and stir my soggy cereal. Mad at my kid for a silly comment born of tiredness and three-ness? My 'mother of the year' application is definitely going to be rejected again.

———

Years ago when Sam was still small enough to sleep soundly at church, our new little family slid into a pew for our parish's penance service. As we settled in, Franco eased his arm around my shoulder with a smile, both of us happy to be out of the house, a rare evening accomplishment with a newborn.

Then the priest started preaching about the place that real reconciliation happens. That too often we hurt those within our own home most deeply. That our need to seek forgiveness starts with our own family. That the reason we come to church for confession – or any sacrament, for that matter – is to help us learn how to live out this grace at home.

The proverbial pin-drop silence in the packed church made me realise I wasn't the only one who felt his words hit home.

A movie montage of the past few months flashed through my head: all the nights I lost my temper at my husband, all the mornings I begrudged my baby his need for nursing, all the sharp words I'd tossed at my sainted mother who spent weeks helping us after Sam's birth. The transition into motherhood proved tougher than I expected, and parenting seemed to hold up a mirror to my every flaw.

I looked down at the sleeping baby next to me in the pew. How was I ever going to get good at this?

———

When I tuck Sam in for his nap, he flips around on his pillow and turns toward me, a worried look clouding his blue eyes. 'Mama, what would happen if I would say, "No, Mama, I want Samantha!" when you came to get me?'

Round seventy-two, I sigh. How am I ever going to get good at this?

I smooth back the hair from his forehead.

'Sam, you are my boy, and I love you no matter what. And I'm so happy that you love Samantha, too. But it's good to love lots of people, and you don't want to hurt someone's feelings by saying you don't want them around.'

He considers this carefully. 'Mama,' he continues. 'Why did Thomas have to take a time-out when he hit me after lunch?'

The non sequitur mind of a preschooler, I smile inwardly. 'Well, Thomas was frustrated and needed to calm down.'

But suddenly I see the dots he's connecting: the hurt he caused and the hurt that was done to him. I remember words about how reconciliation begins and ends at home. I realise that I've been going about this all wrong.

The question is not how to get good at parenting – or marriage, or any other relationship under the family roof. The question is how to grow in love. Of course we're going to keep hurting each other: unintentionally and intentionally, mildly and deeply, once and over again. This is sin's truth, and we're smack-dab in it. But grace and forgiveness can soften our hurts, even slowly help them to heal.

Is this how God welcomes me back, every time I push away in anger or confusion or selfish pride? I had no idea of the depth of forgiveness it takes to love a child. To keep forgiving beyond the small aggravations and the deeper hurts.

So I pull Sam back into my lap. I forgive him, again and always, in the nap time hush of his quiet room. I forgive him with an extra book to read and another song to sing and one more snuggle before I go.

I forgive him, and I forgive me, remembering the rightness of how it feels to reconcile out of love. And I close his door carefully behind me, leaving it open just a crack, just the way he likes it.

BAD MOODS AND BREAKING BREAD

> *[Jesus] said to them, 'When you pray, say: Father, hallowed be your name.*
> *Your kingdom come.*
> *Give us each day our daily bread. And forgive us our sins,*
> *for we ourselves forgive everyone indebted to us.*
> *And do not bring us to the time of trial.'*
>
> Luke 11:2–4

It started off as a lovely morning. Until. Isn't that the way it always goes?

Until the baby smeared yogurt all over his third outfit of the morning. Until the preschooler dawdled away all our free minutes pushing fruit around his plate. Until one child cried for help getting shoes on the right feet while the other tipped over my tumbler of tea and the dog howled for help and suddenly everyone was wailing and white-hot anger surged through my body, tight and hard and shaking and ugly, and I found myself screaming at the top of my lungs, *I cannot DO this, God, I cannot DO THIS!*

Finger-snap fast, the bright sunny morning is brooding and dark. We're sulking in the car and I'm racing through red lights and both boys are sad-quiet in the back seat. All I can think is *this is not how I want to live.* Yelling at my kids and running late and stress pounding through my temples. I take a deep breath, two, three. I ask for forgiveness.

I promise I love them. I sing a song to cheer the mood.

But all morning long the sullen memory lingers.

I pray as I stroll Thomas down sun-dappled streets. I plot ways to ease the morning crunch. I plunk down five dollars at the bakery for Sam's favourite loaf of fresh bread. And then we're driving home, and the car is full of school-day chatter and happy-baby babble and I am overwhelmed with the rush of love and joy and guilt and fear that sweeps over every day of mothering. *God, I love them so much* and *they're such sweet, small things* and *I hate my rotten temper* and *I hope I'm not ruining them.*

Rare is the day that comes easy. But how I wrestle with the days that come hard.

At lunch's end, I pull the loaf of still-warm bread from the paper bag. The moment feels sacramental. I tear off a hunk and offer it to the boy I screamed at hours earlier. He grins and accepts. I do, too.

We both chew, quiet and content. I think about Eucharist. Does it help us forgive? Liturgy and sacrament classes swirl in my head; I can't remember a single connection. But it feels good to slow down and break bread. That much I know.

Before nap time we snuggle with a pile of favourite books. As Sam dives under the covers, he asks if we're going to do prayers next. I start to say no, that prayers are for bedtime, and then I hear my own words. 'Of course,' I reply. 'Let's pray.'

He launches into 'Our Father ...' and I hum along, half paying attention. Until.

Give us this day our daily bread, and forgive us our trespasses, as we forgive those who trespass against us.

Bread and forgiveness, I realise. There it is. I swallow back the lump in my throat and kiss his mop of hair as he turns away on the pillow.

What we need daily: bread and forgiveness. That much I know.

EVERYDAY SACRAMENT

THE GIFT OF THE PILGRIMAGE

The Lord has freed you from your sins. Go in peace.

Rite of Penance

As we board the plane, prodding small boys down the crowded aisle and bumping every seat we pass with the Sherpa-sized packs strapped to our shoulders, the old adage weasels annoyingly to mind: *it's the journey, not the destination.*

Impatient for the endpoint, I shove aside the cliché as I stow our carry-ons under the seats. I'm more focused on getting the four of us to point B in one piece rather than enjoying the ride.

But as we fasten our seatbelts, I still find myself forecasting how this flight will unfold. As always Sam will curl into Franco's arms with the awkward fold of lanky boy limbs into father's lap. By the time we reach cruising altitude they'll be sleeping soundly, both of them scrunched against the unforgiving plastic of the plane's curved wall, heads tipped back in heavy slumber, arms hanging heavy at their sides.

Sure enough, when I look across the aisle shortly after takeoff, they're already snoozing.

Thomas and I? We're another story.

My roommates had dragged me onto the bus to Paris before I had the chance to protest, 'But I'm not a hiker!' in my non-native tongue. For weeks leading up to Lent they had insisted that the Palm Sunday hike from Notre Dame to Chartres Cathedral was no mere romp through the French countryside but a tradition among young Catholics, a chance not to be missed during my year abroad. So they scrounged up an extra sleeping bag, promised me an unforgettable pilgrimage, and I soon found myself surrounded by hundreds of French youths, plodding on dirt roads through bright yellow safflower fields and trudging on cobblestone streets through tiny country towns.

But halfway through day one, what seemed like an inspired idea to start Holy Week on pilgrimage turned into a harsh reality check. My feet were rubbed raw from blisters, my shoulders screaming from an overstuffed pack, my muscles throbbing in places I never knew existed. Only fifteen kilometres in, I decided this was a lousy waste of a weekend. I wanted to hail a cab and go home.

Thomas fidgets constantly in row 36, thrashing to find some comfortable spot on my lap where he can relax into sleep. Whenever he does start to doze, he startles himself awake and starts to howl in protest at the cramped conditions. I resort to ridiculous plea bargains to the Almighty in exchange for twenty consecutive minutes of shut-eye, but instead we're stuck together for hours sans sleep.

The promise of a pleasant family reunion has winged us away this week, but the dreamy vacation is now starting to resemble an outer ring of Dante's *Inferno*: a cranky, sweaty toddler kicking in my arms; strangers glaring across the aisle whenever my son shrieks; my own stomach starting to turn as the turbulence rattles. At my most desperate point, I clasp Thomas's clammy cheeks in my shaking hands, ready to plead something irrational like 'JUST GO TO SLEEP!' when I realise I'm staring into my own dark eyes.

EVERYDAY SACRAMENT

After a long day of hiking, our band of pilgrims collapsed in a cold stone church to celebrate Mass en route. A bishop with a beaming face welcomed the tired crowd sprawled across the cobblestone floor. Afterwards a young priest announced that confession would be available. My roommates slowly scattered to relax outside, and I was left alone sitting at the steps of the altar. Empty chairs stood near the makeshift confessionals, so I figured why not and stepped forward.

When I sat down behind the screen, I was astonished to find the bishop sitting across from me. Trying to keep my cool, I started stumbling through my confession, only to halt when he leaned over with a smile and said, 'You can feel free to speak in English if you would like.' I was doubly shocked.

As I fumbled to start over, the gentle invitation in his voice made something shift inside me. Suddenly I found myself baring my soul to this stranger, telling him about a hurt I had held for years, a burden I'd carried for so long on my own that I never expected to share it with another person as long as I'd lived. The whole story came pouring out, and when I finished, I wiped my eyes on my grimy sleeve and peered up at the bishop, embarrassed at my unexpected emotion.

He looked back at me intently. Then he leaned closer to speak a single sentence: 'Forgiveness will be the gift of this pilgrimage for you.'

The truth that our long flight confirms is that Thomas and I share the same temper. From the early days of his babyhood I suspected this unfortunate fact. While his brother Sam was a fairly easygoing infant, only fussing when he was hungry, tired, or sick, Thomas would flare up out of sheer frustration – racing from quiet calm to red-faced hollering in seconds.

To make matters worse, my temper tended to boil over at precisely the same moment. We made quite a pair whenever our moods got the better of us. I would sometimes catch a glimpse of solemn Sam on the sidelines, sucking in his breath as he watched his brother and mother prepare for a battle of wills, eyes narrowed and locked in our tantruming tête-à-têtes.

Of course, the only beauty of sharing our temperament is that I understood his triggers and tendencies, too. When his temper would rush to the surface and he'd start screaming and kicking to make his protest known, I knew what to do to calm him down. With a kiss and a cuddle and a quiet moment together, his temper could simmer back down as quickly as it had sparked into flame.

But when he can't sleep and I can't sleep and the plane is stuffy and the flight has hours more to go, my defences fall to the wayside. All I can see from beneath my furrowed brow is our family paired off by personality. Across the aisle sits the laid-back twosome slumbering in each other's arms. Here in my seat stews the hotheaded duo angry and awake.

Two of a temper. Heaven help us.

Forgiveness will be the gift of this pilgrimage for you.

That was all he said. No questions, no judgement, no rote penance of three Hail Marys. Just the simplest statement of faith. A reminder that there was no hurt too heavy or guilt too deep to separate me from God's love. A recognition that the peace I sought was waiting once I forgave myself and the person who had wronged me. An affirmation that God was walking beside me as I blistered my heels on this hike.

We sat in silence for a moment. Forgetting every act of contrition I learned in grade school, I stumbled my way through 'thank you' and 'merci' after he offered a blessing, and I turned to leave.

Air travel with small children tends to reduce parents to their barest and brittlest. Faced with Murphy's law that everything that can possibly go wrong, will – from diaper explosions on takeoff to upset stomachs on descent – we are forced to face our own limits. It's no wonder we resort to throwing granola bars or gummy treats at the situation spiralling out of our hands.

But for me it takes an especially hellish flight to make the truth crystal clear: everyone involved in this journey is human and must be pardoned accordingly. Whenever I wrestle to rein in chaos I cannot control, I forget that parenting is not about arriving at some far-off destination, unspoiled and intact. I forget that raising kids is not a performance but a practice. I forget that the only way to forgive anyone else's shortcomings is to forgive my own.

I forget that journeying together and forgiving each other go hand in hand.

I sat for a long time in the quiet hush of the medieval church, watching shadows flicker off the stone walls from the altar awash in candles. I thought hard about the pilgrimage that brought me here and the surprise of a confession I never meant to make.

For the rest of the hike, through whipping wind and sudden rainstorms and gooey mud that caked on my too-tight boots, the bishop's words pulsed in my ears. Sweaty and weary,

I wound my way through Chartres's medieval streets amidst a jostling throng of pilgrims singing and waving leafy branches to celebrate our Palm Sunday arrival. For a moment I pulled away from the crowd, dropped my pack to the ground, and plopped onto the corner of the cathedral steps to lean my back against the cool stone wall.

In my mind the bishop's words still echoed like a refrain: *Forgiveness will be the gift of this pilgrimage for you.* His wisdom was the whole of the Christian journey, it seemed. A long, winding walk in the way of Christ who is love and forgiveness.

And here I was, finally. On the threshold of arriving.

After too many hours, peace descends on row 36. Right when I'm ready to throw in the towel on travelling with children, now and forever, Thomas's tired head of soft brown curls finally lolls onto my shoulder in quiet defeat. He sleeps long and hard as my limbs fall asleep beneath him, buzzing with prickly pins and needles. But he desperately needs this rest, and I reconcile myself to him by not shifting while he slumbers. He is, after all, the child of my own heart. Of my own temperament.

As his breath slows into calm, I remember that this is how reconciliation feels for both of us. The release of forgiveness. The peace of acceptance. The settling back into loving arms.

I smooth back the sweaty curls from his forehead, and I kiss him goodnight. I whisper a prayer of thanks. While he sinks into deeper sleep with each heavy breath, I imagine how many more times he and I will have to practise forgiveness. We who share this temper, this strength of stubbornness and spunk, must also trudge the long road of learning what it means to reconcile. With each other, with ourselves, ultimately with God.

Perhaps forgiveness will be the gift of our pilgrimage, too.

CHAPTER FIVE

Helping to Heal – Anointing of the Sick

KNEADING HANDS

> O Lord my God, I cried to you for help, and you have
>   healed me.
> O Lord, you brought up my soul from Sheol,
> restored me to life from among those gone down to
>   the Pit.
>
> Psalm 30:2–3

I'll call her Mary. The undoer of knots.

I first met Mary in the dark winter when I was pregnant for the second time. As snowy wind whipped across my face, I stumbled through the glass doors of the glowing salon, knocking dirty slush off my boots onto their welcome mat.

'I'm here for a massage,' I mumbled to the receptionist, her highlighted hair swept up into a perfect bun. She barely glanced up from her computer as her manicured nails tapped the keyboard. 'I'll tell Mary you're here,' she said breezily, turning to answer the phone.

Then around the corner came Mary, plodding and plump, smiling behind thick glasses and mousy brown hair. My heart sank. This was not the strong masseuse I pictured when I made the appointment: the muscular therapist who would work my aching limbs into the pinnacle of health. But nothing about this freezing winter – or this difficult pregnancy – had been what I expected. What was one more disappointment?

Oblivious to my pessimism, Mary welcomed me warmly. I followed her to the salon's back room, where she dimmed the lights and drew back the sheets on the massage table. As she stepped out to let me get ready, I wrestled out of my clothes and shivered as I slipped under the blanket. I lay waiting in the dark, hoping that the next hour would ease my throbbing back now tugged by the growing belly that stole my sleep.

Little did I know Mary was about to help heal something deeper.

Mary's hands were stronger than her petite, pudgy frame would suggest. She was unrelenting in her pressure, digging her elbow into the deep of my back, kneading her knuckles into the knots of my neck. Once or twice I almost yelped when the pressure bordered on pain, but her fingers sensed exactly when to pull back. Hers was no wimpy squish of shoulders; this woman could work miracles in muscles.

When the hour had passed, she laid her hands lightly on my shoulders for a moment. 'You're all done, honey,' she said softly and slipped back out the door. After I dressed in the dim room, I blinked back into the bright light of the salon's foyer. I caught a glimpse of myself in the mirror behind the reception desk: my hair greasy from massage oil, my forehead splotched with lines from the face cushion. I looked like hell.

But as I drove home through the black frost of February, sore and sweaty, I felt softened, like something tight inside me had loosened for the first time in months.

To call this pregnancy hard was an understatement.

After the euphoria of learning we were expecting again, I slipped suddenly into the vertigo of morning sickness. Or rather, all-day vomiting that proved to be a much fiercer foe than the first trimester woes I'd experienced before. One dark night I found myself curled on the couch, shivering beneath a heap of blankets, unable to keep down a saltine or a sip of Gatorade. Franco frowned as I feebly argued that I'd be fine, fading in and out of awareness. He finally insisted on telephoning our clinic, despite my weak mews of protest.

Upon hearing my condition, the on-call doctor prescribed anti-nausea drugs and warned that if I didn't keep some food or drink down in the next few hours, he would admit me to the hospital. I barely remember seeing Franco rush out to the twenty-four-hour pharmacy across town to pick up the medication, but later I raised half an eyelid to find him next to the couch, dropping one white pill into my hand. I let it dissolve on the back of my tongue, and then drifted back to fitful sleep.

By morning I was able to cough down a cracker. My bloodshot eyes wearily met Franco's as the sun rose pale through the window.

'You're going to be fine,' he assured me. 'I'm sure that was the worst of it.'

We had no clue what was coming.

———

Every time I called to schedule another massage with Mary, I felt guilty. Just one more, I chastised myself. With another baby on the way, what was I doing wasting money at a salon? Splurging at a time we should be scrimping. But I craved the comfort of her hands.

As my hormones soared and belly swelled, Mary adjusted to my changing body with grace, plumping extra pillows around my middle, changing techniques to let me rest on my side. When my own bed grew too uncomfortable for me to sleep soundly, I could still rest undisturbed on Mary's table. Her small studio became a sacred space. Each time I entered, I felt like I was coming home.

One stormy Saturday while Mary worked on the stubborn throb in my lower back, I started weeping without warning into the foam pillow where my forehead rested. Her hands paused in surprise. 'What is it, honey?' she asked, leaning over the table toward my face. 'What's wrong?'

Where do I start? I wondered as I snivelled. The doctor's dismissal of the darkness I'd tried to describe? The therapist's daunting diagnosis of prepartum depression? The miserable loneliness I was hiding from family and friends? Or the desperate fear that I didn't deserve to love this child within me?

'It's everything,' I finally managed to say. 'I just feel so overwhelmed.'

'Oh honey, I know,' she said, rubbing my tense shoulders sympathetically. 'Being a mom is the roughest job around. It's so much work; it never ends. That's why you have to take better care of yourself.'

How many other moms had tried to share words of encouragement with me? But this woman had placed her hands on my body, literally touching me where I felt most broken. Hers was a rare blessing.

Trapped in the cold, dank bottom of a pit called depression, I sat stuck deep within darkness I couldn't climb out of. If I prayed at all, I pleaded for help to get out of this hole: *'To you, O Lord, I call; my rock, do not refuse to hear me'* (Ps 28:1). I tried to trust that in the back of my shadowy mind I could scrape together enough crumbs of faith to outlast the present darkness.

Only later would I learn what a common burden I was carrying, that at least one in ten women experience depression in pregnancy. But during those awful months I felt only alone.

Until I felt another's touch.

Unlike the sterile clean of the doctor's office and the cold instruments he used to measure the baby's growth, Mary's welcoming studio pulsed with the earthy scent of the lavender oil she rubbed into my skin. Whenever she laid her warm hands on my sagging shoulders, I began to breathe deeply again.

When my friends seemed too distant to reach and I couldn't bear to pick up the phone, Mary held my hands and rubbed smooth oil into my cuticles chewed raw from worry. As she carefully slid out my limbs one at a time from beneath the warm white sheet, she poured out attention on each arm and leg, down to the tired fingertips and toes. Even as the world seemed dull and daunting beyond the fog that clouded my vision, I heard life crackling around me as Mary's wooden massage table creaked beneath me while she worked. Her ordinary gift of hands laid on my hurting body, of hopeful words spoken over suffering, of oil spread across my skin that held a deeper ache – all of this was healing when I needed it most.

———

The last time I saw Mary was three weeks after Thomas was born. After the long slog toward his delivery day, I was practically euphoric in the postpartum phase, even as I inched my still-healing body gingerly onto her massage table. While we settled in she asked to see baby pictures, hear the birth story, and commiserate at the challenge of going from one child to two. As she rolled up her sleeves we started chatting about her mother, who, it turned out, worked for thirty years at the same hospital where I'd just given birth.

'She loved working on the labour and delivery ward,' Mary said as she poured a small pool of oil between my shoulders and started to rub it into my back. 'She said she just loved every day of that work, seeing the new moms and the babies. She said it didn't feel like a job – like it was almost a gift, you know?'

I did.

A few months later I called the salon to treat myself to another appointment with Mary. I missed our chats, and I especially missed her miracle-working on my shoulders. 'Oh, didn't you know?' the receptionist chirped.

'Mary left the salon.'

I felt like I'd been punched in the gut.

'No. Really?' my voice trailed off as I traced the worn edges of Mary's business card on the kitchen counter.

'Yeah, she wanted to be at home with her kids. She'd tried cutting back her hours but then she decided that she wanted to be with them full time.'

I tried to smile a little, to be happy for her. But now I'd never get to say thank you. Or goodbye.

'Did you want to schedule an appointment with our new therapist?' the receptionist prodded. 'She's great; I'm sure you'd love her.'

While I considered her question, I absentmindedly rubbed the back of my neck. It felt soft and strong, nowhere near as tense and knotted as it had been a year before when Mary first laid her hands on me.

'I guess not,' I replied, straightening up. Surprised at the certainty in my voice.

'But didn't you need a massage?' she asked again, confused.

'No,' I said, glancing down at little Thomas, napping blissfully in the bouncy chair in the corner of the kitchen, his long lashes fluttering onto plump cheeks, his tiny lips half-smiling as he slept. I thought about Mary, wherever she was, never knowing how our hours together had changed me, how much tension her hands helped release, how holy her touch had been, how much longer the dark months in depression's pit would have dragged if she hadn't been there to help pull me up.

But here I was now: up, out, beyond. Safe. And grateful.

'No, I don't need another appointment,' I finally said to the receptionist waiting for my response. 'I guess I'm okay now.'

And as I hung up the phone, I realised for the first time that I was.

THE WOUNDS WE HOLD

But we have this treasure in clay jars, so that it may be made clear that this extraordinary power belongs to God and does not come from us. We are afflicted in every way, but not crushed; perplexed, but not driven to despair; persecuted, but not forsaken; struck down, but not destroyed; always carrying in the body the death of Jesus, so that the life of Jesus may also be made visible in our bodies.

2 Corinthians 4:7–10

Thomas's knee is skinned and raw, a jagged line of gravel from the driveway sliced through his skin in deep diagonals. He cries so hard he can barely breathe, his squinched-up face turning splotchy pink as the cuts start to seep bright red. I hustle him upstairs to the bathroom as he heaves angry sobs – 'My knee! My knee!' – and set him down on the toilet seat cover as I turn to open the drawer for the plasters.

But he panics at the thought of my leaving and lunges out to grab me, slipping off the seat and bumping his knee on the edge of the tub, sending his screams an octave higher. The white tile is now streaked with blood and dirt. I wheel back toward him, nearly dropping the plasters and pulling him into my arms. He gulps for air in howls, and I try to comfort him with shushes. My T-shirt is wet with his tears, and his blood smears crimson stains across my shorts. But I will not notice these until later, until I have quieted his cries enough to set him back down and daub his cut with a warm washcloth to clean out the stony dirt. Until I squeeze out ointment to spread a thin layer across the deepest cuts. Until I shake out a stack of plasters from the box and peel one from its plastic casing. Until I line up the soft centre of the bandage on his bleeding knee and gently press the two sides down on his skin with my thumbs.

Already I see the blood soaking through the gauze, but at least it is covered. At least he is quiet.

I look up at Thomas, his dark round eyes still streaming silent tears toward his chin. I lay a hand on his bandaged knee.

'I love you,' I tell him, leaning forward. 'It's going to be OK.'

I don't know how she did it.

I remember the big plastic tub of hospital-grade supplies on the upper shelf in our upstairs bathroom, the spools of gauze and rolls of medical tape, the dark brown bottles of iodine stocked to dress my brother's wounds after the surgery that removed a third of his pelvic bone. I never saw my mother peel off the strips of worn tape or pull back the giant square of gauze that covered what must have been rows and rows of angry stitches. I was too young to watch, of course, and never one with a stomach of steel. I could barely bring myself to glance at the contents of that bin every time I went digging for a plaster for my own skinned elbow or blistered ankle.

I don't know how she did it without a nurse's training or a doctor's expertise. Maybe that capacity for care comes once cancer moves in. Or maybe this is what years of love let you do: peel back a pus-soaked bandage, wash the raw wound, pat the screaming skin dry, apply the antibiotics, place clean gauze with a tender touch and unwind strips of sticky tape to secure the dressing. Then sweep the mess – the proof of the pain and the tests and the diagnosis and the prognosis and the chemo and the radiation and the surgeries – with one swift swoop into the wastebasket with a smile. And a quick kiss on his forehead before he ducks away in that smiling teenage way: *c'mon, Mom*.

Maybe caregiving teaches you to anoint this way: to put your fingers into the wounds and to hold the bleeding pain in your hands. Or maybe it is parenting itself that teaches us to love in the body, this body we hold from first bath to first falls, this body we bless with kisses and plasters, this body my mother could not heal but kept anointing, this body she finally had to let the coroners lift onto a cold gurney and wheel away from her home forever.

I do not know how I would do it. How I would love like that.

And yet I do not believe this road ends anywhere else but the altar of unexpected suffering. We lose control of our lives once a baby is placed in our arms, and we do not let go of love even when the pain is too great for us to bear.

But maybe we, too, are anointed along the way. Maybe we are blessed by the God whose hands touched lepers' sores and blind men's eyes and feverish children and bleeding women. Maybe we, too, are given some sliver of peace, promised that there will be hope if not healing, relief if not remission, comfort if not cure. Maybe we are strengthened against the fear and the doubt, the grief and the anger that eat away at our insides. Maybe this is how we become Christ's hands for each other.

I do not know. I cannot know what cuts this calling will ask me to tend, or what deeper wounds I will only be able to hold in prayer. But I do know that the tender acts, the simplest acts, the sacred acts of pressing skin to skin and blessing with our touch – that all of these – are holy. That God is present even when we are powerless. That God is whole even when we are broken.

WHEN THE HEART BREAKS OPEN

Through this holy anointing
may the Lord in his love and mercy help you with the
*   grace of the Holy Spirit.*
May the Lord who frees you from sin save you and raise
*   you up.*

Rite of the Anointing of the Sick

We'd timed the pregnancy perfectly. I took a test one sunny morning. We held the stick up to the window and smiled to each other. The line was faint but positive. We treasured the secret to ourselves. The next week I took another test, just for fun. Even darker. I made an appointment with the doctor and stocked up on Saltines for morning sickness. We spent a weekend deep cleaning the house before first trimester exhaustion took over.

The week before my appointment I took one last test, just to be sure. This one we'd officially celebrate with Sam and Thomas over ice cream that night. I cheated and let my eyes dart to the stick on the counter before two minutes were up. I was sure the proof would be instantly dark.

It was not.

Only a slight line. A shadow of what we'd seen before. Franco came into the bathroom, straightening his tie for work as he glanced down at the countertop. His brow furrowed. I bit my lip. *It's not supposed to be like that*, I said in a small voice, looking up at him with watery eyes. He stared down again. We both knew.

I called the doctor's office and asked to come in that day. My test in the clinic was negative. The nurse frowned and said they'd run another. Maybe there had been an error. Negative again. She quickly swept the pregnancy handouts off the bench where I was sitting.

The doctor thought my dates were wrong; maybe I was weeks earlier than I thought. I knew I wasn't; we'd been charting for years. She ran more blood work. Low levels of the pregnancy hormone turned up. She thought this was proof of pregnancy. A trace of hope. I lay awake in bed that night staring at cracks in the ceiling, knowing it was not.

The next morning I kept worrying that I would see blood. I tried to tell myself it was silly. Maybe the doctor was right. I tried to pray. I tried to work. Before lunch I went to the bathroom one last time. I looked down. Bright red blood pooled everywhere.

The rest of the day blurs into a daze. I cry. I call Franco at work. I try to walk the dog. I go back inside and try to eat lunch but can't. I tell the sitter I'm not feeling well and I'm going to work upstairs in the bedroom. I try to rest. The cramping tightens suddenly, turning into contractions. I call Franco again and tell him to come home now. My arms and legs start to buzz like pins and needles. Suddenly all four limbs go numb. I crawl to the phone and dial the doctor. The triage nurse interrupts to say that I should get to the ER immediately. When Franco walks through the door I'm clawing the blankets on our bed. The contractions pound in waves. I can't gasp to speak. He carries me out to the car. I wail like a wounded animal the whole drive to the hospital. The same drive we first made exactly four years ago that night, when I went into labour with Sam.

All I can think as we race down the highway is *it wasn't supposed to be like this.*

We squeal up to the same drab brick entrance, only this time there are no labour and delivery nurses waiting to whisk me away in a wheelchair. I stagger through the sliding doors on Franco's arm and collapse into a plastic chair while he runs to find a nurse. Someone leads me through the emergency room doors. The nurse taking my vitals asks for my birth date, and I struggle to remember. There are multiple doctors and more nurses and too many questions and blood draws and ultrasounds. And waiting, so much waiting, waiting for hours, waiting as the contractions finally start to slow and let me breathe again, waiting for labs and tests and results and confirmation of what we already know.

Which is that six hours later we are walking out of the hospital, the same hospital where I birthed both my babies four floors up, leaving this time with nothing but a plastic bag of sanitary pads and a prescription for painkillers.

It wasn't supposed to be like this.

Two weeks later we managed to get to church, late and harried. I sat through Mass mostly numb, trying not to tear up at every pregnant woman who waddled through the communion line. At the end the priest announced there would be a healing prayer afterward by members of the parish prayer team. Maybe they offered this regularly, but I had no idea what it meant. I started to pack up the kids' jackets and books, but Franco raised his eyebrows and bent over to whisper, 'Do you want to go?' I stared at him, puzzled for a minute about what he meant. But then I felt a strange nudge.

Try it.

I had no clue what to expect. As the crowd scattered for the parking lot I walked up to the woman sitting in the corner of the church. I sat down in the chair across from her and told her I'd never done this before. I took a deep breath and told her I had a miscarriage. I started to cry. Her eyes looked like sad pools of grey behind her glasses. She cupped my hands in hers and asked, 'Can I pray for you?' I nodded. She closed her eyes, so I did, too. And for the next five minutes – or ten or twenty, I lost track – she wove words around me like a shawl. Words of comfort and healing, words of compassion and hope, words of support and community, words of love and motherhood. I wondered where she learned to pray like that, to let it flow out of her so smooth and warm. I didn't want her to stop.

When she finished, she asked if I would like some holy water. I pressed my knuckles into my eyes to stop crying and said OK. She dipped her fingers in the small glass bowl on the low wooden table between us and traced the sign of the cross with water in the centre of each of my palms. It glistened like tears. I walked back down the empty aisle of the church, my hands and eyes still wet.

A few weeks later they offered healing prayer again after Mass. This time I hesitated. The empty chair in the corner sat facing a man with a bushy beard. Suddenly I wasn't sure if mine was the kind of grief only women could understand. Franco nudged me back to reason. 'You should go again,' he said. 'You said it helped last time.'

Of course he was right. Sympathy didn't come from similarity. I sat down in front of the man and simply said, 'I had a miscarriage.' He nodded, dropped his dark eyes to the floor, and started to speak a prayer with the beauty of a poem. I watched as my tears dropped black dots of mascara onto my white pants. I didn't care.

Maybe it wasn't an official anointing, a sacrament blessed by a priest, but here in this quiet corner of our church, strangers were holding my pain. They sorrowed with me: *it wasn't supposed to be like this*. They turned over my palms and smoothed a blessing into the creases of worry. They lifted up my head from the ground of grief and spoke grace into my red-rimmed eyes. Their words were oil and their hands were holy.

All of this was more than enough. It was God poured out.

Part III
CALLINGS: MARRIAGE AND HOLY ORDERS

Callings begin. The question starts quietly, even in childhood: What will I be when I grow up? We imagine our way into professions, relationships and identities. Each dream unfolds with an inkling of an invitation, a spark of a suggestion. We try and test; we wonder and wander. The idea of a calling suggests a clear voice, one that will wake us in the night and tell us where to go, but God's call is often much quieter: an inner whisper, a gentle nudge, a stirring within that invites us to consider what our life's love and work may be.

Callings continue. Every sacrament is a call from God and an invitation to respond. But the sacraments of marriage and holy orders (ordination to become a deacon, priest, or bishop) celebrate these particular callings as a way of life. Both sacraments are professions of vows that seal a promise of faith; both start in a celebration at church that leads into a lifelong commitment. The way we view these two vocations reflects how we understand the many callings in our lives that, while not explicitly sacramental, are also deeply sacred: parenthood, professional work and every other path by which we respond to the world's needs through loving service.

Callings change. Vocations evolve over time. Within one couple's marriage are many different stages; within a parent-child relationship are numerous phases; within any professional career or priestly ministry are multiple shifts. We are transformed by the commitments we make. Life's challenges redefine what we thought our callings meant, but God remains faithful through the changes, inviting us to continue listening for God's call to new life.

Callings ring out. The bells that peal after a wedding or an ordination are only the beginning of what marriage or ministry will mean. These vows rank among the most public declarations of faith: how we have chosen to commit ourselves for the rest of our lives. But no matter the kind of calling we respond to, we open ourselves to sacramental and self-giving love. The work and relationships that make up our callings become a central part of our identity: for better or for worse, our lives are defined by our response to the calls we hear from others and from God. We become connected to each other through the ways we work toward the common good – of our families, our communities, and the society in which we live.

Callings echo. Sacraments of calling need regular reminders and repetition long after the initial profession of vows. For a married couple or an ordained priest, practising the daily reality of marriage or religious life is what keeps their vocation alive. While a wedding or an ordination may rank among the most extraordinary moments of a Catholic's life, these sacraments become the most ordinary: the foundation of our identity and our daily work. And no matter what sacred path

God calls us to follow, we are invited to enter into the vision of a life in which every day is holy.

CHAPTER SIX

Everyday Vows – Marriage

THE FOCAL POINT

This is my commandment, that you love one another as I have loved you. No one has greater love than this, to lay down one's life for one's friends.

John 15:12–13

'And that,' he declared dramatically, thrusting out his arm behind him, 'that is what marriage looks like.'

From where I was sitting near the altar, poker-straight in my gown's white bodice, I turned to where the priest pointed and saw what I had stared at every Sunday of my childhood. A looming wooden cross with a crucified Christ, his limbs lifeless and his head bowed low.

Marriage looked like that?

'Ask any couple married more than five years, and they'll tell you it's true,' the priest continued in a booming voice as a few nervous chuckles tittered from the pews.

'Marriage means death. Marriage means sacrifice. Marriage means the mystery of laying down your life and rising to something new.'

Theologically, I thought I understood what he was saying. The cross was supposed to be front and centre for every sacrament. But practically speaking? This blushing bride hadn't spent too many hours pondering exactly how suffering was going to shape our happily-ever-after.

He went on with his homily, but I kept staring at that crucifix, its slender wooden beams, its carved sinews of a body heavy in death. I couldn't shake the idea that marriage looked less like us, the fresh-faced couple eager to take our vows, and more like the tortured Christ hanging on the cross above us.

Hours later at the reception, over clinking wine glasses and laughter spilling out from the dance floor, a family friend asked what I thought of the priest's homily.

'Pretty weighty stuff for a wedding,' she offered as she raised her eyebrows over a plate of hors d'oeuvres. 'By the end I couldn't even follow what he was saying.' I swirled a sip of champagne as I wondered how to respond. Because the troublesome truth was that I'd promised 'I do' to exactly what he described. To the cross at the centre of our new calling.

Whenever Franco travels internationally for work, I struggle with solo parenting. Two- or three-week stints overseas have become routine for his engineering work, but I never get used to the challenge of enduring long stretches with no relief pitcher walking through the front door at dinner time.

If I'm honest, my real angst behind his adventures abroad is not the exhaustion of running ragged or the annoyance of caring for the kids and household solo. It's that his travels always make me face my deepest fear: that I will lose him. My overactive imagination conjures up fantastical catastrophes – a jetliner crashing into the Australian coast or a freak car accident on a dusty Indian highway or a rare disease caught in a crowded Chinese market. In the days leading up to his departure, as he's stuffing his suitcases with clothes and I'm cramming our calendar with distractions, I find myself flooded with morbid thoughts: *What if this is the last dinner we have together? What if this is the last time we sleep in the same bed? What if something happens to him while he's gone? What if something happens to us?*

Irrational fears. Or perhaps the most rational human fear: that what we love will be taken from us.

Yet once he's gone, self-preservation mode kicks in. I find myself focused on everything but him. The kids who cling to me even more than usual, clamouring for the attention of two parents. The errands and chores that all fall on my to-do list. The house that fills with clutter and unfilled bills. When he calls to check in, I can be curt. Glad to hear his voice and grateful that he's fine, but still stuck in my selfish woe-is-me mode.

This is the hardest part about his absences: spending all day with my own unchecked ego. Hiding from fears that he won't make it home and I'll be left to flounder on my own forever.

***

On this latest round of travels he's gone for most of June, working in Australia for three long weeks. My mother-in-law graciously offers to take the boys one Saturday so I can get out of the house by myself. I gratefully accept. Perhaps too eagerly, I squeal out of the driveway with a wave, revelling in the sheer silence coming from the back seat.

I turn onto the winding road that follows the river to a small-town yoga studio. I feel so frazzled with work and kids and house and chores that I know I need ninety minutes to relax and recentre on what's most important. Which I suspect is not the grimy stove covered with dirty pots from three straight dinners of mac-n-cheese, or the disaster of a home office I haven't had a spare second to organise, or the four looming loads of laundry that threatened to smother me as I slipped out the back door. By the time I step down the cold concrete stairs to the warm basement studio, I'm ready to collapse onto my mat.

The yoga class does my tired body good. I stretch and reach and feel my limbs strengthening as I hold a challenging pose longer than I think possible. Maybe I can do this. My mind relaxes, too. Deep breathing helps loosen my grip on the frustrations I've been clenching since Franco has been gone.

As the class nears its end, we turn to balance work. Normally these poses are one of my favourite parts of yoga, but today my legs feel shaky. I try to perch like a flamingo, tucking my left leg into the crook above my right knee, but I can't seem to find the sweet spot to steady myself. The teacher notices my teetering.

'Pick a focal point,' she reminds us. 'It will help you keep your balance.'

My eyes concentrate on a tiny crack in the wall in front of me, and I take another long breath. As my gaze steadies, I feel my feet sink slightly into the mat, finding a firmer grounding. I start to lose myself in my focus. This is the point, I remember: to look out beyond myself and stop worrying about the wobbles. To discipline the mind and strengthen the body.

That's when I realise: the cross is the focal point for my marriage. The centre that steadies my shaking.

Christ makes this sacrament make sense.

On one level our lives are maddeningly out of balance right now. Franco is ten thousand miles away and I'm juggling two kids, a busy work schedule, all the household chores and the normal life crises that spring up unplanned. But if I can keep centred on the cross as the focal point for our marriage, then the rest of my callings fall back into right relationship with each other. I focus more on the kids right now, knowing that once he comes back we'll redivide the duties more equally. Work won't feel as crunched when I can catch up on the weekends, and the house will one day be clean again. Most important, the partner I chose for my companion will be back home where we both belong.

When I remember that this calling is about sacrifice, then I unclench my frustration and soften into open palms. When I remember that this sacrament teaches us to bend low in love and rise up together, then I turn back toward the spouse I've promised to honour. When I remember that this marriage was never just about us, that we were never sent off alone to make this life a reality, then I welcome back the God who was here all along and ask for the help we need to love each other well.

If I keep my eyes fixed on the cross as our focal point, I can steady my wobbling spirit.

———— ✦ ————

Ever since we were married, a crucifix has hung on the wall in our bedroom. Deep brown wood, polished to smooth, a gift from my parents. A friend once glanced up warily as she passed through our room. 'Isn't that morbid?' she joked. 'To have a dead guy hanging over your bed?'

I thought about telling her how many times I've had to lay down my own selfishness at the altar of this marriage. Or how surprising forgiveness feels each time we reconcile back together. Or how learning to love for the long haul takes daily practise in dying and rising.

But I stopped myself.

'Actually it's not so creepy,' I replied, thinking of the priest's wedding homily from years ago, the unforgettable fling of his arm toward the cross, the deep green of his chasuble robe pointing to Christ, the unsettling words that became a mantra for our marriage, a meditation on loss and love.

'It helps keep me focused.'

I DO. AGAIN.

*According to the Latin tradition, the spouses as ministers
of Christ's grace mutually confer upon each other the
sacrament of Matrimony by expressing their consent
before the Church.*

Catechism of the Catholic Church, 1623

My father's parents were married in Indiana during the
Second World War. On an early Saturday morning in May
1942 my grandmother Katherine finished the final exam of
her junior year at Saint Mary's College, and then walked over
to join her groom Raymond at Notre Dame's Church of the
Sacred Heart. Even before it became a basilica fifty years
later, Sacred Heart spread a stunning backdrop for a nuptial
Mass: soaring arches, dazzling gold altar, and star-studded
ceiling of deepest blue.

My mother's parents exchanged their vows in 1938 at Our
Lady of Mount Carmel, a small country church in Wickliffe,
Ohio. The wedding was simple and small, fitting for the post-
Depression era: a morning Mass and a modest meal afterwards
at the home of the bride's parents. Black-and-white silent
footage shows my grandma Betty grinning underneath the
brim of a wide hat, showing off her wedding ring outside the
church steps before she and her new husband Roger ducked
into the car to speed off down the dusty dirt road.

Franco's grandparents were wed worlds apart: one set in
Italy, one pair in Minnesota. Narciso and Assunta celebrated
their wedding in April 1936 among rolling Tuscan hills in a
local Catholic parish near their hometowns. Following Italian
tradition, the bride wore a black dress, still technically in the
traditional mourning period following her father's death

two years earlier. Laurence and Virginia were married at a small Lutheran church in rural Minnesota on Thanksgiving Day in 1941. Two weeks earlier, Virginia had announced the engagement to her mother, and then borrowed a wedding dress from a friend before the newly married couple headed south for an exotic Iowan honeymoon.

My parents held their wedding in my mother's suburban Cleveland parish, the Church of the Gesu, on a warm and sun-drenched Saturday in October 1969. They walked behind the communion rail – a lingering vestige after the Second Vatican Council – to exchange vows that echoed off the church's marbled walls. Filling the pews were two big Catholic families and the wedding party of fourteen that stretched across the photos that my siblings poured over as kids, marvelling at the world before we existed.

Five years later, Franco's parents walked down the aisle in the Church of St Timothy – a neutral compromise since Alfiero's home parish of St Patrick's wouldn't fit Susan's extended Minnesotan clan. So the Italian Catholics and the Scandinavian Lutherans together packed the church and Knights of Columbus reception hall to raise a cup of punch to the happy couple, she in her hand-sewn wedding dress and he in his dapper 1974 tuxedo.

Franco and I got married in my childhood parish in Michigan, the same brown brick church where I received every other sacrament – baptism, First Communion, reconciliation, and confirmation. The same church where I'd watched my sister walk down the aisle and wondered when I might take my turn. The same church where I'd heard this priest and that organist and these hymns echo off the wooden ceiling beams a hundred times before our big day. But contrary to all the faded photos and the marriage certificates and the family stories, these churches – from Michigan to Minnesota to Indiana to

Ohio to Italy – weren't the places where each couple finished taking their vows.

They were where we started saying, 'I do.'

———— ⟋⟍ ————

Sometimes I sift back through these stories, when the day has been dragging and there's still so much to do after the kids are tucked in bed. I wonder what it meant to say 'I do' in a poor corner of Tuscany or a lavish basilica in Indiana. Proverbial wisdom says that if all these pairs hadn't promised their vows and kept renewing them with each long day, then we wouldn't be here. But there is more than mere biology that shaped how our stories wove together. Each marriage is a constellation of ancestors and influences: parents, grandparents, siblings, friends.

Our family trees and photo albums are living proof of how a sacrament is a communal reality, not an individual creation.

The real beauty of these stories – how the weather unfolded, who was invited, what unforgettable memory emerged – is how these tales are only the beginning. When each bride and groom walked back down the aisle arm in arm, the I-dos were only starting. Because even when a priest is present to witness the vows, and popular parlance says 'the pastor married us', the bride and groom are themselves the ministers of the sacrament. And wisely so: we marry each other – technically, theologically – because we have to keep marrying each other.

We will repeat these vows every day of our lives.

———— ⟋⟍ ————

I'm exhausted. Do you want to get up with the baby next time he cries? *I do.*

Thanks for cleaning the house while I was gone. I hope you know how much I appreciate it. *I do.*

I have to work late again, so we can't hang out like we planned. I hope you know I'm disappointed, too. *I do.*

We have a million errands to run this weekend, but do you want to see if my mom would watch the kids on Saturday so we can have a date night? *I do.*

Our vows are ongoing. This is how we practise: with daily repetition.

You really want to drive twelve hours through the snow to my parents' house for Christmas? *I do.*

I've been thinking about going back to school. I know our calendar is already crammed, but do you think we can make it work for one night a week? *I do.*

Maybe we're ready for another baby. Do you think we should? *I do.*

Our vows are affirmation and action. This is how two grow into one: we say yes and we live out yes.

When the kids are sick with a week-long stomach bug, *I do.*

When we're both worn out from long weeks at work, *I do.*

When the basement is a mess and the garage is a wreck and the kitchen floor sticks to our feet from weeks of unmopped spills, *I do.*

Our vows never end. This is the refrain we repeat to verse after verse of marriage's song.

Because the sacrament that shapes the rest of our lives did not end when we smiled our way into the reception hall. We are still, steadily, slowly – maybe always – becoming married.

So perhaps it is not at church but at home where each couple takes their vows. Where we learn what it means to live out the hard truth of our promise. Where we choose each day to embrace our calling all over again. Over dirty dishes and dirtier diapers, over flat tires and fights about finances, over late-night worries and early morning laughter in bed before the kids wake up.

Daily we make our commitment by these repetitions.

I do.

WHERE THE STORY BEGINS

Will you accept children lovingly from God, and bring them up according to the law of Christ and his Church?
Rite of Marriage

The summer that Sam turned three, the balance tipped. On a humid July night we celebrated our sixth anniversary. After we tucked the boys in bed, we snuck downstairs for dinner on the good china plates we rarely use. An elegant meal, the kind we never make when kids are at the table – with elaborate appetisers and homemade salad dressing and pleasant pauses between courses. We listened to jazz glide in from the old stereo in the living room, and I swirled white wine in my glass while I waited for Franco's answers to my anniversary questions, always the same: *What was the best part of the past year? What do you hope happens in the year to come?*

Thomas, he answered to the former. Cop-out, I replied.

Sleep, he answered to the latter. Good one, I admitted. After we piled up the dishes in the sink, deciding that scrubbing dried pasta sauce off plates was not a romantic end to our evening, we crept upstairs to peek in at our sleeping babies, mouths tipped open in deep slumber, damp curls matted across their foreheads.

As we slipped into bed with warm night breezes fluttering through the curtains, I thought back to how far we'd come since our wedding. Grad school, job changes, two babies, two moves. We were in the midst of becoming the grown-ups we always laughed we'd never be.

That was when I realised the scales were about to tip. For an instant our marriage was teetering in the balance between the years with children and the years without. From this point on, the days when we were partners but not yet parents would start to recede in the rear-view mirror, slipping into a far-off memory like sleeping in past nine or spontaneous date nights.

Two halves of one marriage. One that was becoming more about them and less about us.

———— ∽ ————

I loved the years of early marriage. Of course we had to work through annoyances and adjustments to living together, like every couple does. We argued over finances and household chores and whose turn it was to clean up the dog's latest accident. We had to learn how to fight and how to forgive, when to hold on and when to let go. But still we jumped into married life with joy at having found our partner.

We shopped for furniture to fill our new house and dug up half the yard to try our hand at a vegetable garden. We got a beagle and took him for long walks around the neighbourhood. We emailed each other at work with date night ideas and met at uptown restaurants to enjoy long laughs over dinner. We split dessert but never the check.

So when becoming parents proved harder than planned in the midst of those lovely early years, it was tough. Scratch that: overdone steak is tough; algebraic equations are tough. Infertility is just plain awful. It is depressing and upheaving and gut-wrenching, a knotted twist in a couple's story. You slam up against your own limits and find yourself powerless. You can do nothing but try and hope and pray and wait and see.

One sunny spring day after we'd been trying to have a baby for a year, my college roommate called out of the blue to tell me she was pregnant. I tried my hardest to be happy, but as soon as the call ended I stared down at the phone in my hands and started to sob. Franco came up the stairs from the basement to find me weeping on the top step. He pulled me into his arms while I wailed. 'It's never going to happen for us – I'm so happy for them and it's never going to happen for us. We're never going to have a family.'

'No,' he said to me, emphatically. I pulled back in surprise, still sniffling. 'We are already a family. Don't ever forget that.'

He was right, of course. But still we wanted more.

For us, infertility eventually ended. But our daily reminder of the sheer blessedness at the chance to have children has wrapped our experience of parenting in awe and gratitude that fundamentally changed our marriage. Once paused for an instant between the pre-kids and post-kids eras, I saw how our love – this imperfect, still-trying, somehow-sacred love – had become the birthplace of our babies.

Our marriage was where their stories began.

Watching your partner grow into parenting is a strange and moving thing. I have moments where I catch myself staring at the boy I smiled at across that crowded dance floor at the college bar a decade ago. I wonder how on earth we got here, how he's scrubbing yogurt off a high chair, trying to tell me about his day at work while a whining toddler clings to his leg.

The carefree years of young-and-in-love seem far away now that our days are full of care: for them, for work and home, for each other. But this is how love spreads. It starts with two and flows outward.

The night before Sam's birthday that summer, we finally hung pictures on the walls of our new house. One of the first was our wedding photo. After Franco expertly engineered the levelling of the frame, we stepped back to admire his handiwork, late afternoon sun reflecting our silhouettes onto our younger selves behind the glass.

'Did they let us get married when we were sixteen?' he laughed. 'We look like kids.'

I drifted back to that sunny Saturday in July. The scent of stargazer lilies filled my nose, now from a slender vase on the counter instead of a round bouquet in my hands. I thought about the two halves of our marriage: the spontaneity and simplicity of pre-kid days and the turning point of a baby's arrival that changes everything. I realised that the further we get from our wedding day, the more our marriage becomes something bigger than those two goofy kids grinning in the frame.

Our story is changed by the life we bring into this world through our love.

CHAPTER SEVEN

Challenges of the Calling – Holy Orders

A LITANY OF THE DIRTY WORK

Think of us in this way, as servants of Christ and stewards of God's mysteries.

1 Corinthians 4:1

O toxic diaper pail, whose staggering fumes plug my nose as I rush you to the garbage can outside
O crushed crackers, whose dusty crumbs cower with stale Cheerios in corners of the car seats as I chase them with the vacuum nozzle—
O mysterious stains, whose sticky rings under the table tempt trails of ants in steady streams to whatever spilled at yesterday's snack—
Housework. Chores. The dirty work.

It's a humbling start to every morning: unload the dishwasher, scrub the sink, set out stacks of breakfast bowls, start the washing machine churning, fold the first load from the dryer, scribble a grocery list, and drag the recycling bin outside. All before the kids start to stir upstairs.

It's a tiring end to every evening: fill the dishwasher again, scrub the pots, wipe the counters, sweep the kitchen, sort the mail, fold two more loads of laundry, toss the last trucks in the toy bin, and pay a stack of bills. All before crawling into bed.

The long list of each day's to-dos becomes my weary litany: the washing and the folding, the cooking and the cleaning. Tired protests mutter through my head as I spin dizzy round the kitchen, arms full of art projects and magazines and bills to file or fling into the trash: *not what I went to college to do, not worth my time, not part of my calling.*

The work we do behind closed doors is unglamorous, often unnoticed. Parents do what must be done out of duty or a desire to seek order in the constant churn of chaos that family life leaves in its wake.

What could ever be holy in this?

———

O speckled bathroom mirror, whose streaky surface is splattered with toothpaste sprays and water spots from bath-time splashes—

O scattering clods of dirt, whose thrilling flight from the toddler's mud-caked sneakers has dragged the vacuum back from the closet moments after the entire carpet had been scrubbed clean—

O sodden shorts, whose darkened colours betray the soaking wet that almost made it to the potty, which now must be peeled off little legs and flung dripping into the hot wash cycle—

Is there ever anything holy in housework?

When I was twenty-two, I slung a giant backpack over my shoulder to spend the year after college in France volunteering with the Sisters of the Assumption. Part of my placement was to serve as an assistant in a L'Arche community, a home for adults with developmental and physical disabilities. I had zero experience with this work, so I had no idea what to expect, beyond glowing pictures of meaningful service to people in need. But when I showed up the first morning and introduced myself, the head assistant in the house told me that for now, I'd be doing the laundry.

The laundry?

She led me down the cold concrete stairs to the dank basement, part of which still served as a root cellar with dirt floors. In the corner room, lit by two thin windows covered with cobwebs, laundry lines crisscrossed overhead, draped with sopping wet bedsheets. We ducked under the maze and stepped over the puddles pooling on the floor to find the ancient washer and dryer. She showed me where the detergent was kept, how to gather up dirty clothes from the residents' rooms, and what schedule they typically followed for the week's laundry.

And then she added, as we turned back to walk up the stairs, 'You'll have to iron it all, too.'

Iron?

I had always loathed ironing, what I considered an entirely pointless affair. You spent twenty minutes pressing crisp corners into the arms of a shirt, and then it wrinkled as soon as you put it on and sat down in a chair. My approach to laundry was both lazy and pragmatic: if it couldn't be tossed in the dryer to tumble dry the wrinkles, I wouldn't wear it. I'd never imagined spending hours sweating over a creaking ironing board with a towering pile of T-shirts, shorts and fitted sheets at my feet. All of which were shoved squarely into my category of absolutely-useless-to-iron.

But this was standard house procedure. And this became my daily task. To pull armfuls of sheets off beds first thing in the morning, sheets soaked with urine and reeking of worse, and transform them by afternoon into a smooth stack of freshly pressed replacements in the linen closet.

I hated it. I hated every minute of it. I grumbled to myself through the steam and sweat for the first few weeks: *Was this what I came all the way to France to do? Iron stupid sheets? I'm supposed to be serving people. That was the whole point of this year. What a waste.*

EVERYDAY SACRAMENT

But one clear fall day as yellow leaves streamed down from the backyard tree outside the window, I looked up from the hissing iron to realise where I'd been doing this work all along: right in the centre of the house. Between the living room and dining room was the only space where I could fit the ironing board, so every day as residents gathered downstairs before heading off to their work sites, I stood there in the centre, ironing.

Each morning I would chat with Angelique and Stefan while they ate their morning cereal and *chocolat*. I took good-natured teasing from Benoit about how I folded his pants wrong. I once asked Dominique if she wanted to start sorting the socks and her eyes glowed with pride at the invitation to help.

Suddenly I realised this might be exactly where my service was supposed to start. With the ironing.

Maybe there was something sacred in the housework after all.

O elusive dust bunnies, whose small grey tumbleweeds of dog hair always escape my broom across the entryway—

O steamy dishwasher, whose groaning whir hums through the whole morning catching up on crusty pots and pans abandoned after last night's dinner—

O late-night vomit, whose pungent aroma turns my stomach as I try to wipe every trace from the wooden crib slats and the beloved stuffed animals—

Years after I left L'Arche, I still have to remember this truth over and over: how the dirty work can be holy. It's an easy lesson to forget as endless repetition wears you down over days and weeks and months. I have to seek inspiration elsewhere to keep cleaning as the chaos keeps coming.

So now as I hang up dripping bath towels and scrub grimy toilets and wipe down spaghetti splatters from the microwave door, I think about the calling to the priesthood.

Maybe it seems a strange solidarity to seek with celibate men without children or a dual-career household to manage. But I imagine a priest could lament the same way about the dirty work of his own vocation: *O headaches of parish administration, O stacks of budget paperwork, O teeth-gritting mortgage negotiations, O never-ending personnel politics.*

Perhaps he dreamed of ministering to people or sharing the sacraments or preaching the Gospel, but whatever inspired his ordination was quickly overwhelmed by other tasks: *O joy of overseeing construction projects, O thrill of fundraising for new sound systems, O wonder of racing between parishes to celebrate Sunday Mass, O delight of constant interruptions from emails and phone calls and after-hours knocks on the rectory door.*

But pastors, like parents, grow into the truth that tiresome tasks are part of the service that springs from love.

Parenting has taught me this about priesthood: what it means to be a servant leader. You do the dirty work that no one else wants to do. You work hard and you stay up late. You don't seek success on the world's terms, but you stay faithful to the love that first inspired you, even on the exhausting days. Because dirty work is what makes the relationships possible, which are at the centre of the calling.

Sometimes we think we choose vocation. We decide to pick a profession, or get married, or have a baby, or take religious vows. But along the way, the calling claims us, too. With all its hard work and thankless duties and late nights. With all its wandering and wearying and wondering if the sacrifices were worth it. I've learned that most parents – and most priests – will always tell you yes. A deeper litany of gratitude echoes underneath the grumble of the daily grind.

EVERYDAY SACRAMENT

Maybe this is where God speaks in whispers as we work: over heaps of laundry, under dishes clattered in the sink, through cries on the baby monitor. Over debates about decorating the church for Christmas, under piles of notes for unwritten bulletin columns, through midnight calls to bless an emergency surgery.

Core to every calling are responsibilities that exhaust us. But if my litany of chores begins and ends in love, then wearying work becomes its own practice of prayer. Even when the orders do not seem holy or the to-do list inspiring, this humbling repetition can still be an everyday sacrament of godly work.

Of God's work, too.

SHOWERED WITH BLESSING

The Lord bless you and keep you;
The Lord make his face to shine upon you, and be
  gracious to you;
The Lord lift up his countenance upon you, and give
  you peace.

Numbers 6:24–6

'Surprise!' we smile, pulling our friends into the dining room.

Ice-filled pitchers of lemonade and iced tea sit sparkling in the Saturday afternoon sun. Shiny presents with bright bows wait poised for their spotlight moment. Maybe it's not the most air-tight of surprises, since our reunion weekend together has been brimming with baby talk, peppered with questions of what gear to buy and how to find childcare and whether to hire a doula for delivery. But the parents-to-be are all good enough sports to act surprised, to indulge us in silly shower games, to ooh and aah over teeny onesies and sturdy board books.

It's no small miracle. I look around the table at three of my closest friends from college and each one is expecting: five months along, four months, two months. The surprise showers we plotted over email as the announcements arrived – first one, then two, then an astonishing third revealed just this weekend – have blended into one big baby celebration. A couple's shower times three.

We roommates, who used to spend hours regaling each other with epic stories from last night's party, now chat about nursery décor, confer about prenatal testing and compare the best brands of bottles as we sip virgin versions of our favourite college cocktails. Franco laughs as their husbands open gag gifts we schemed to include the dads-to-be: a Star Wars diaper bag, a hipster onesie with tattoos, baby football gear to cheer on our alma mater. We all toast to the head-shaking wonder of sharing pregnancy together.

But even in the sunlit afternoon bursting with laughter, even while our own boys nap peacefully upstairs, my heart sinks quietly. We lost our baby only a week earlier. I can't shake the thought that for the briefest glimmer of a moment, all four of us had all been pregnant together. Franco catches my eye from across the table and I know he's thinking the same thing.

Their joy is complete, but ours tastes bittersweet.

———

Parents-to-be aren't the only ones whom we bless at the beginning.

When Sam was nearly two, we watched one Sunday as a new priest, a native son of our parish, celebrated his first Mass of Thanksgiving. Michael had grown up in the congregation, attended its school, and returned to the community throughout his years in seminary. So his homecoming after ordination felt like a family affair, spilling beyond his proud parents beaming in the front row. As I jiggled my curly-haired toddler on my hip, I nudged his attention toward the altar: 'Look at the brand-new priest!'

At the eucharistic prayer the newly minted Fr Michael was encircled by a crowd of fellow priests: a slew of seminary professors, priests from the diocese who had served as mentors, and the pastor and associate pastor from our parish. Standing behind him around the marble altar, they all stretched out their hands – some weathered and wrinkled, some young and smooth – to bless with him the gifts of bread and wine. And as he spoke the sacred words of consecration, their voices – some soft and low, some bold and strong – blended with his own as he lifted up the chalice and host for the first time.

As Sam's legs wrapped around my round pregnant belly, the scene we watched suddenly struck me as strangely familiar. Young and old gathered together, proud smiles and hopeful faces, loved ones and dear friends. A mix of generations, a circle of celebration, a symbol of support. One person's new vocation standing at the centre of attention.

Then I realised. If I only swapped the genders and switched the backdrop to a crepe-papered living room or a flower-filled backyard patio, it would look just like a baby shower.

Here were the beaming faces of those who had gone before, who had birthed the same dream into reality. Here were generations who shared years of experience in the same calling, blessing the baby steps of the journey, reaffirming this sacrifice of love. Here was one young person beginning anew the ancient task, the adventure of a life's work.

Of course there were no piles of pastel presents waiting around the altar. No games of 'baby bingo', no glasses of pink sherbet punch, no fawning over tiny outfits bedecked in zoo animals. But maybe the same instinct gathered the brotherhood of priests and the sisterhood of mothers: the need for nervous novices to be surrounded by wise ones whose presence affirms they are not alone.

But baby showers are bittersweet, too. We forget when we draw up the invitation list that our parties are never the pure festivities they appear. Ringed round any cheery banquet room are friends agonising through infertility, relatives waiting on adoptions, mothers who suffered miscarriages, aunts who let dreams die when they never married. They sip their coffee and smile through pleasant conversation, but inside the same struggles stir up once more.

If I had looked closer that Sunday, peering into each pastor's eyes as they blessed the eager new priest, would I have seen some slight hesitation dart across one face, a hint of shadow in his glance? Odds are on that altar stood priests whose calling had brought them unexpected suffering. Or who wrestled with demons of doubt. Or who knew the pain of dreams deferred.

Perhaps they looked at the fresh-faced young man before them and wondered what might be his own cross of the calling, what crucible moments would tremble his hands and seize his throat. Surely they wished him well and prayed him courage, but they knew it would not be easy.

They knew that when you open yourself up to love, it can break your heart.

———

A priest's path is no different from anyone else's, full of twists and turns, detours and dead ends. This is the nature of vocation: we respond to a call without knowing where it will lead. But this does not mean the road is not right or the life we have chosen is not holy. It simply echoes the truth that the wise grandmother at the baby shower and the white-haired pastor on the altar know so well. That no love is free from pain. That control is an illusion. That callings lead back to the cross.

Back when I was seven months pregnant with Sam, sitting in my sister-in-law's lush backyard, smiling under the summer sun at my own baby shower, unwrapping hand-knit blankets and plush baby toys, I never dreamed that opening up my life to motherhood would eventually find me mourning a miscarriage in a cold ER triage room. You never believe at the beginning that the new calling you've embraced will one day break your heart.

But no novice can grasp this truth in its entirety. Energy, enthusiasm, and eager expectation blind the beginner – mercifully, maybe – to the daunting task ahead. When I think of all the parents I know, rare is the family whose beginning was born without heartache. Instead there are babies lost to miscarriage or infertility or stillbirth. There are babies born too early or babies born too sick. There are babies conceived unexpectedly or babies that followed in overwhelming succession. And all the babies who arrive healthy, hoped-for and on time – they turn their parents' world upside down, too, by the simple fact of their neediness, their unrelenting demands, their exhausting vulnerability.

Yet what makes a calling holy, whether a priest's orders or a parent's duties, is the depth of commitment that is confirmed as we discover strength and trust we didn't know we had. This is how God calls us, how Christ companions us, how the Holy Spirit blesses us – not just to inspire optimism at the outset, but to carry us through the challenges along the way.

That sunny Saturday as I sat round the gift-wrap-strewn table with my pregnant friends, I realised that each one would encounter her own heartaches as she grew into parenting. No one could protect them from this loss. All I could hope for them was the same prayer I whisper whenever someone sets out on a new calling: to know love, to be love, and to grow in love. This was my small, silent plea between sips of lemonade and bursts of laughter. That love would carry them through the calling when nothing else could. That love might keep carrying me, too.

Showers are sweet send-offs, beautiful as a blessing from an altar. But after the thank-you notes have been written and the new baby clothes folded into waiting drawers, this is how a vocation gets deepened and seasoned: through struggle, through suffering, and through sacrifice. All we can do at the bright beginning is surround one another with support. Bless each other with the hope that God's grace will bring peace. Strengthen those beginning with the promise that they will never journey alone.

EVERYDAY SACRAMENT

TO MY CHILDREN, CALLED IN CHILDHOOD

May God who has begun the good work in you bring it to fulfilment.

When we were waiting for each of you to be born, your father and I picked out your names. I scribbled possibilities on the back of meeting agendas; he tossed out ideas over dinner; we kept a running list on the laptop as we debated each other's suggestions. When it finally came time to choose, we agreed on names that we loved. Names of personal significance, remembering relatives that we cherished. Names of theological meaning, echoing saints and scriptural figures we respected.

But equally important? Names that could be nicknamed.

This was no toss-away afterthought. This was a deliberate decision born of two parents whose first names were never easily shortened by classmates or coaches, nothing like the Christophers and Katherines in our classrooms growing up. Since every parent is condemned to compensate for what they feel they lacked (a *mea culpa* you may someday know yourselves), we were naturally drawn toward something different. Names that had multiple alternatives. Names that could change between school and home. Names that could grow from baby days into adulthood.

Samuel, Sammy, Sam. Thomas, Tommy, Tom.

Perfect, we thought, for each of you. Names full of possibility.

But then a strange thing happened. People around us started doing exactly what we'd intended – calling you by variations on a theme – and it turned out we weren't as wild about the idea as we'd expected.

For our first, we intended to hold onto the full 'Samuel', savouring the promise of its biblical meaning – a long-awaited child whose parents prayed to God for him. But after a few months, we discovered that you were simply a Sam. The nickname began in babyhood and stuck. Or so we thought. Until one side of the family still insisted on calling you 'Samuel' and the other side delighted in dubbing you 'Sammy J.' And there we were, your father and I, left digging in our heels as your name slipped out of our grasp.

Turns out that we who signed your birth certificate in the hospital room weren't in control of what you were called.

For our second, we loved 'Thomas' – stately, solid, and strong as the daring disciple who questioned Christ to deepen his faith. This time the full name fit, even in the lisping mouth of your older brother. But then one branch of the family tree leaned toward 'Tom' and the other was inclined to make a matching pair with 'Tommy A.' As before, no one seemed too concerned with our parental preference. So we shrugged. Once again out of our control.

Lessons linger from this business of naming. About our plans and dreams and the reality they meet. About the illusion of control over the souls we help bring into this world. About the power of being called by name – through all its variations, in multiple directions, by many different people who love and need and claim us.

The truth is that who calls you, and what you are called, and where you are called, has the power to shape your life and your identity, even beyond your parents' wildest expectations.

What does it mean to have a calling?

Perhaps you would protest the very thought of a vocation. (As is your *modus operandi* to protest everything in these early years.) Perhaps if you could grasp what a calling could mean, what a weight it might have on your life, you would shove it away like one-too-many kisses from a doting mother or yet another bemused glance from a patient father. Yet I can tell you each with certainty that you are called from birth by the God who created you, and you are claimed from baptism by Christ whose name you bear. Called to be and to do. Called to follow in unexpected ways.

A crazy idea? Perhaps by the world's standards. But here is where I want to challenge conventional thinking on the subject.

Vocation is not reserved for the mature and the adult. Each of you is called from childhood, beginning as the young sparks you are. Here and now, you are sons and siblings. You are grandsons, nephews and cousins. You are classmates, friends, and neighbours. You are on the way to becoming – something and someone more than we could ever imagine today. But you are also called as you are now. Your vocations are already and not-yet.

What you will become remains a mystery. Perhaps this is refreshingly and terrifyingly true for all of us, no matter our age. But childhood lends itself to dreaming, even by the adults around you. Each time one of you dives into a new interest or reveals another talent, those who know and love you leap to speculate on what you might become. An engineer for your fascination with cars. A lawyer with your penchant for arguing. A mathematician for your love of numbers. Whether these passions evolve into vocations, only time will tell. For now we wait and wonder.

But certain moments make us stop and take pause.

When you two were wriggling worms at two years old and two months young, we watched together in the cathedral pew as the seminarian who baptised Thomas became a priest. As I whispered in your ears to keep you quiet through the hours-long Mass, we listened to the bishop pray over the newly ordained: *May God who has begun the good work in you bring it to fulfilment* (Rites of Ordination).

At that exact moment, Sam, you scrambled out of my reach. You lifted high above your head the hymn book you'd been flipping through, and started to carry it solemnly around our pew. The elderly couple behind us chuckled. Your dad elbowed me and grinned, rolling his eyes.

But your gesture caught me in the throat, clichéd though it may seem.

A mother's head is always full of dreams of what her babies might become. But until that moment, with a baby teething on my shoulder and a toddler taking his procession out to the aisle, I had never actually pondered the possibility that the priesthood could be your path. Maybe you will indeed feel called to follow Christ in this way, carrying around your own Book of the Gospels to the pulpit to preach. (Or maybe you just wanted to whack your baby brother in the head with a heavy hymnal.)

But watching the two of you there in the pew at church, among a community I hoped would nurture whatever callings would be yours, I realised that for each of you there will be sacrifice and service and holiness in your vocations. Whether you become a parent or a priest, whether you pursue a profession or forge an unconventional path. Through the gifts you will be given and the needs you will be shown, you will continue to be called into life by the God who walks with each of us.

———

When I was pregnant for the first time, your Aunt Deirdre wrote me a letter with a few words of advice on surviving the newborn days:

The gift I most want to pass on to you cannot be gift-wrapped. It is the idea of 'portability'. I took my kids everywhere as babies. We spent hours in the National Gallery and Natural History Museum, hours in Starbucks, too. I took them to nearly every park in the city, wandered neighbourhoods I didn't know.

As infants, they were obviously far too young to 'get' anything from these outings. But they had massive value to me as a new mother. They made me put my babies (especially my very small one) out in the world, and made me realise very early on that they were part of something much bigger than I was.

So my biggest advice is as soon as you have your sea legs, get your baby out. Take him to the places you love. Take him on hikes in those beautiful woods and take him to your amazing art museum. It will make you remember that you are a person, not just a parent, and that goes a long way to having a healthy, loving baby.

Take your baby out into the world. I remembered those words long after all the advice that a first-time mother hears – Let him cry it out! Never let him cry! Wean him early! Nurse him till he's two! Stay home full-time! Get back to work! – finally died down.

But even as her words echoed in my ears, nudging me out the door with a newborn to the park and the playdate and the library, I still couldn't see clearly what I know now: that hers would be the best advice I'd receive on parenting. Because she reminded me that my calling as a mother is to introduce you to the wide world and the God who created it, so that I can help each of you learn how you are called in turn.

Called to take your place, to share your gifts, to serve in the ways you will be shown.

———

Sceptics sometimes ask what I will do if you grow up and leave the Church, or if you don't believe in God. (This, I fear, is only one of many occupational hazards you will encounter in having a theologically minded mother.) Then won't all of this have been a failure – all these years of trying to nurture you in the life of faith?

Not at all, I respond.

If I can raise you to know that you were created by God, loved beyond measure, and called to share your gifts with those in need, then I believe this understanding will stay buried within your bones, no matter which road you choose. Your journey may wind into church or out of church, but wherever you go, it will be within the wide embrace of God who changed the essence of existence by love. My confidence in that truth runs deeper than any parental fears.

This is why I can heed your aunt's wise words, to take each of you out into the world and help you sniff out the beginnings of whatever trails will lead you on. Because I know that you are not mine to keep forever. You belong to God, and you belong to God's wild world. So I can whisper these hopes with confidence – when I wake you in the morning to pull you sleepily into another day, when I drop you off at school to learn and play, when I answer your unending curious questions of why, when I tuck you in at night with songs and prayers. *May God who has begun the good work in you bring it to fulfilment.* This is the same prayer I hold for you, Sam, and for you, Thomas. A prayer of trust and hope and gratitude.

And this is the same prayer I cradle for you, too, the child whom I carry below my heart. The one we have been waiting and praying for. The one who will arrive with spring's green buds and warm breezes. The one who today is kicking and fluttering and quickening into being. Our baby of new hope and second chances, of life after loss. You who will soon have your own name (nickname-able, of course) and your own callings, full of wonderful possibility. You who call me into motherhood again, beyond my fears.

To each of my children, I give thanks. For the gifts you have been from God. For the people you are and the people you will become, loved and called by many names. For the vocations you will discover and the communities you will serve. For the painful and joyful ways you birth your parents' vocations into being. For the gifts you call forth from us and the needs in the world you open our eyes to see.

And for all the ordinary ways you make our daily life together holy – this sacred chaos, this messy grace, this everyday sacrament.

In Gratitude

Authors often compare writing a book to giving birth and they thank those who helped as midwives through the painful process. For me the experience of writing this book has been more like caring for a newborn: staying up too late, waking up too early, pushing to the brink of exhaustion yet still delighting in this new creation God blessed to bring to life. I am deeply grateful for all those whose support carried me through this arduous and wondrous work.

For the unabashed cheerleaders in my family, especially my parents. For the staff of Liturgical Press who welcomed this idea with open arms. For Mary Nilsen, whose teaching helped me to claim writing as a calling and whose editing made this manuscript infinitely better. For the Parents with Pens writing group, whose support gave the inspiration I needed. For the PQ, whose boundless enthusiasm always believed I could do this. For Genevieve and Deborah, who have been my MDiv companions across the miles. For Sr Angelo Haspert, OSB, whose spiritual companionship guided this book long before I started to write it. For Kathleen Cahalan, with whom it has been a privilege to work on vocation for these past five years. For the communities of Notre Dame and Saint John's, especially the School of Theology and the Collegeville Institute, who opened my heart and mind to theology's questions. For the parishes of Saint Andrew and

Saint Joseph the Worker that have nurtured our family over the years.

For Franco, who helped make all of this possible. For all the Saturdays you gave me to spend writing. For all the nights you let me disappear into the office while you cared for the boys. For your unfailing love, your unwavering support, and your true partnership.

And for our children: all four of you whose lives shaped this story. You are the greatest and most humbling gift I have been given. May God's everyday love continue to grace our lives with joy, now and always.